Redempti

So

ISBN: 3-9808084-6-7

Yema Lucilda Hunter

Redemption Song

While the war in Sierra Leone was on the author's mind when this book was written, hence the cover illustration, it is a work of fiction. Events, names of people, places, and reference to any matter in this book are coincidental.

First published 2006
Sierra Leonean Writers Series / Africa Future Publishers
c/o Binty International Ltd.
P.O. Box 30265 KIA
Accra, Ghana

Acknowledgements

I am extremely grateful for the valuable insights into this kind of conflict gained from Professor Paul Richards's book *Fighting for the rain forest (1996)*. I am also indebted to my husband, Kobi; my children, Jessie and Mark; sisters, Imodale, Smita, and Velma; my dear friend, Nance Mjamtu-Sie; and my publishers, who read the manuscript at different stages of its development. If I have finally produced a novel worth reading, it's thanks to their frank comments and useful suggestions.

siren's deafening blast.

Malick, who was serving a two-year sentence, stepped through the imposing black gates of the prison a free man again, eighteen months after that conversation. He immediately started working towards his goal by successfully smuggling small quantities of locally grown marijuana into Europe. A business trip to South East Asia which exposed him to even more lucrative possibilities made him add heroin to his illicit merchandise. And when he realised the fabulous returns on even modest amounts of cocaine, he included that banned substance to his secret inventory as well.

For two or three years his fixed deposit bank accounts grew as steadily as beer guzzlers' bellies, then luck deserted him. He was on the point of establishing his own team of drug couriers when, as he passed through the customs hall at a British airport one fine spring morning, police dogs out on a random patrol, sniffed cocaine on his shoes. That misfortune was the result of a visit to a clandestine drug packaging workshop on the very day of his overnight flight. Before he could collect his thoughts or make any protest, he was hustled away in handcuffs and into a white van with blacked out windows.

Malick's arrest led to another, much stiffer jail sentence, but consoled by the knowledge that his well-hidden wealth was still secure and growing, thanks to the interest on his savings accounts, he almost succeeded in shrugging off the sentence as a providential rest stop. Of course, it helped that the British prison system tried harder to reform convicts than the one he had experienced in his own country. He used his time in jail to study for 'O' level maths and passed his exam with credit. The prison authorities never discovered that studying was a mere pastime with this prisoner, or that his exemplary behaviour and professions of remorse were deceptions meant to influence them in his favour. They knocked three years off his ten-year sentence for good behaviour, then had him deported.

Kanekeh, meanwhile, had spent three more years in prison and the eight years after his release drifting along the West African coast by land and by sea. He worked at different times as a ship's cook, a security guard, a middle-man for a rice merchant, a diamond miner and finally, with the help of a bicycle he was able to purchase on credit, as an itinerant supplier of video films for rental. None of these endeavours brought him any closer to satisfying his thirst for revenge and his enemies remained firmly in power. Small wonder then that bitterness had etched grooves on either side of his mouth and cast a deeper shadow over his brooding countenance.

It was at that low point in his life that Kanekeh met Malick again - a chance encounter at the entrance of the Lebanese shop which provided the video cassettes he rented out to clients operating film parlours in the surrounding towns. A large faded sign hanging from the roof of the building, announced to the world in huge blue and red letters that the proprietor of the shop was *Samir Hariri, General Merchant.* On this particular afternoon, having completed his latest transaction, Kanekeh was just about to wheel his bicycle down the two steps leading from a porch to the street, when a metallic grey Toyota Land Cruiser with blacked out windows pulled up outside the shop, raising red dust and crunching gravel on the untarred road.

At the sight of the passenger who stepped nimbly out of the vehicle, Kanekeh dropped his bicycle and risked a twisted ankle in his hurry to reach the new arrival. He cried out, 'I can't believe it! Malick! My brother, is that you...Is that really you?'

Eleven years had gone by since he last set eyes on Malick who, with an equally delighted exclamation, stooped to wrap his arms around his former comrade in adversity.

'Yes, my brother, it is really me. Have you forgotten? This is my home town.'

The two men stepped back and appraised each other for a moment, the way people sometimes do after a long separation. Kanekeh took in Malick's well built form and handsome face with its high-bridged nose and greyish-green eyes, his snakeskin shoes, heavy gold bracelet and necklace complete with embossed medallion. He also noted the perfect fit of his grey safari suit which could only have been achieved by an expensive tailor.

'Look at you!' he said, trying not to betray envy, 'your dream came true-eh?'

Malick responded with a gesture of dismissal.

'Far from it, my brother, far from it. Money is coming, I won't deny that, but far too slowly for my liking.'

'So long as the tap keeps on flowing...' Kanekeh answered. 'After all, you are still young…'

'Young!' Malick protested. 'Soon I shall be fifty.'

'Well, perhaps you were too ambitious,' said Kanekeh.

Disagreeing, Malick replied, 'No, my brother. It's just that I have had a few setbacks.'

Kanekeh raised his eyebrows in surprise.

'Enh!! Well, from what I can see, not many.'

At this, Malick simply laughed and clapped his friend fondly on the back.

'It's been a long, long time,' he said. 'Come inside, let's talk.'

Kanekeh was grateful that Malick seemed not to have noticed his own shabby appearance. Thanks to the rigorous exercise routine he still followed every morning, though chasing fifty himself, his belly remained as flat and hard as a board, and the muscles in his arms like thick ropes. But he was well aware that his much laundered polo shirt and fraying trousers, proclaimed him to be a man with shallow pockets.

Malick led him back into the shop, where Hariri was leaning over the counter, picking his tobacco-stained teeth as he waited for customers. Casually informing him, that he was borrowing the office for a while, Malick entered a back room and beckoned to Kanekeh to follow. Evidently, Hariri had no objection to Malick's offhand manner because a few minutes later, a smiling young assistant arrived bearing a tray on which rested small porcelain cups without handles, containing strong black coffee laden with sugar. By this time, the two men were sitting at a table and as the aroma of the coffee wafted over it, a fiercer pang of envy clutched at Kanekeh's heart. Indeed, this world is not level, he thought sourly. Malick was right. Without money people treated you as if you were a nobody. *He* had been doing business with Samir Hariri for almost three years, yet the man had never once offered him even water in a tin cup. He felt only slightly less resentful when Malick, sensing that an explanation was called for, mentioned that Hariri was his cousin on his father's side.

'So what happened to you after you left 'the big yard?' Malick went on to ask.

'O, I travelled here and there,' Kanekeh replied. 'Travelled and worked for my living. Nothing worth mentioning...'

'And what about what you told me you wanted to do?'

Kanekeh shrugged as he took another sip of the coffee, thinking as he did so that it was just as well that the cups were so ridiculously small. How could anyone enjoy drinking such a syrup?

'I soon realised that getting those people out of power could only be a dream,' he said, feigning indifference. 'And as you know, nothing has changed in this country. The bastards are still hanging on to power as if God Himself gave it to them...Perhaps if I had been able to go back into the army things might have been different - people are really fed up now. They will dance in the streets, I know, if someone makes a coup; but as a civilian and one who has nothing, what can I do? Who would even listen to me? I tried to get money, you know. I mined diamonds for one whole year, but to be honest with you, I could not bear to have my legs soaking in dirty water for the whole day and every day…And as for parasites! Even after I left the washing sites, for a long time I used to feel as if little insects were walking up and down my legs…'

Noticing that a blank look had replaced Malick's previous expression of keen interest, Kanekeh paused, feeling rebuffed again.

Indeed, his friend's mind had wandered along a different path altogether. Though he had been trying not to show it, the more he listened to Kanekeh, the more depressed Malick felt. How could the man be so resigned to his circumstances after talking so passionately about his desire for revenge? By now Kanekeh should have taken some action towards fulfilling his heart's desire, unless that was all it had been - just talk. On the other hand, Malick mused, perhaps Kanekeh was one of those people who needed a push in the right direction as well as plenty of encouragement to get him going. His mind seemed fixed on a military coup, whereas a rebel movement like the ones happening all over Africa could be much more useful. It might lead to a full-scale war, which would open up all kinds of opportunities for making heaps of money...

'Sorry, my brother, sorry,' he said, roused from his reflection by the lengthening silence. 'An idea came to me while you were talking. Carry on; then I will tell you about it.'

'No, no, *you* carry on,' Kanekeh replied. 'I have finished.'

Ignoring his friend's injured tone, Malick leaned forward with his shoulders hunched in a posture Kanekeh remembered well from some of their private conversations in the prison yard.

'My brother, one thing I have learned is that you have to make your own luck in this world. Otherwise, you will stay where you are and even deteriorate. You have to *hustle*...Haven't you heard what is happening in Africa these days?'

'What particular thing?' asked Kanekeh, not quite appeased. 'So much is always happening in this godforsaken part of the world...'

'Rebel movements - guerrilla warfare,' Malick told him.

'Oh, as for that. It is all you hear about on the BBC. Fighting here, fighting there. Displaced people, refugees... They say that man in Libya is the one training people.'

'It is true,' Malick replied. 'And what is more - and I am sure you did not know this - the training is free. All you have to do is go there. People are building up their own armies now. That is what you have to do if you want to pay those bastards back for what they did to you. Build up a small army and kick them out.'

Kanekeh laughed out loud, but with little amusement. Build up his own army! The idea was too ridiculous for words!

'Even if I am able to find the money to go to Libya,' he said, 'how will a poor man like me be able to afford to buy guns, let alone feed a whole army? Sometimes, I can hardly afford to feed myself...'

Malick's cat-like eyes glinted, so focused now that Kanekeh felt as if they could see into the back of his skull.

'My brother, look here,' he snapped. '*Nothing* is impossible if you are determined enough. Nothing whatsoever.'

Thumping his chest to emphasise the point, he went on, 'I have proved it. The only reason those people are still around is because nobody has been determined enough to get rid of them...Do you know how many passports I have?'

Wondering where this seemingly irrelevant question was leading, Kanekeh merely shook his head.

'Five,' Malick informed him with a self-satisfied smile. 'Two of them are under false names and three I got from other countries. I went to jail in UK, you know - for seven years...'

'What!' Kanekeh exclaimed, while interjecting mentally, so *that* was one of the setbacks…

'And they deported me immediately afterwards, but do I care? I go to other countries and do my business without any hassle. You have to know how to *move*, my brother. Otherwise you won't get anywhere-oh. I'm telling you. You can get the training, build the army and throw them out. Just make up your mind to do it... When last did our army fight in any war? Do they even know how to fire guns properly? Do they even have guns to fire? And think how sweet your revenge will be. Those guys will never get over the shame and disgrace of being thrown out - especially if they run to places like England and America where no one will give a damn who they are. Even with all the money they have stolen, they will become nobodies. Nonentities. After all the bootlicking they are used to, it will kill them slowly and painfully - like a cancer spreading in their bones ...'

As he listened to Malick's pep talk, Kanekeh's imagination began to stir like a boa constrictor just finished digesting a goat. Could it be, he wondered, that this chance encounter was the answer to his daily prayer that his enemies should suffer the way they had made him suffer? His heartbeats quickened and he began to feel slightly light-headed, as if his blood were surging through his body with unusual force.

Watching closely, Malick observed Kanekeh's growing excitement. He leant further forward, lowered his voice to a whisper and continued to press his case.

'Listen. I travel a lot - to many countries. I know people who know people who will be ready to make a long-term investment in a project like that. They will help. That I don't doubt. The only thing is, are *you* ready?'

'Of course I am ready!' Kanekeh exclaimed with an air of

reproach. 'How can you ask me something like that after what I told you? You should *know* I am ready...'

In spite of that fierce assertion, Malick continued to harbour doubts about Kanekeh's determination. However, always on the lookout for ways of entering the big league where wealth was concerned, he decided to take a chance with him. The situation in the country was just ripe for a revolution.

'I shall set things in motion,' he said, pushing back his chair. 'Let me have your contact. You will hear from me again… very soon.'

As they parted, he wrapped an arm around Kanekeh's shoulder, muttering in his ear, 'Our future President.'

Having never envisioned any scenario beyond his enemies' exit from power in disgrace, Kanekeh was so taken aback by Malick's suggestion that he stopped in his tracks.

'No-oh, my brother,' he said, sincerity written all over his face. 'I am not seeking that position for myself. All I want is for those criminals to leave this country so better people can take over. Perhaps...'

What Kanekeh had been about to add was, 'Perhaps you know someone who could do the job,' but misinterpreting the speculative gleam in his eyes, Malick backed away, shaking his head emphatically.

'Don't even think of it,' he said. 'Have you forgotten that I have been to jail twice? Who would want to make me president?'

Who indeed, Kanekeh silently agreed, though he was genuinely fond of Malick. Nobody with the interests of the country at heart could possibly entertain such an idea. Malick saved him from having to think of a tactful reply by going on immediately to say that, in any case, he would hate having to put up with security men and bootlickers around him night and day.

'We have plenty of time to think about who should take over,' he added. 'Let us drive these ones out first.'

<><><><><>

Malick's skilful and persistent wheeling and dealing bore the desired fruit. Within six months, of their reunion, Kanekeh found himself in the

Sahara desert discovering that it was possible for his skin to turn several shades darker. He mastered the latest in small arms technology and studied the art of waging guerrilla warfare. He also spent many hours in conversation with aspiring and confirmed revolutionaries he met at the training camp as well as in struggling to understand the 'Green Book' of revolutionary ideas written by Colonel Gaddafi himself. And his muscles grew harder still.

In rare periods of solitude, he would lie on his canvas bunk reflecting on the remarkably smooth way events had unfolded since meeting his former comrade in adversity again. In the end, he came to the conclusion that the hand of God was in it. Once that idea took hold of him, his original desire for revenge began to seem petty and soon gave way to a much higher purpose. He now saw himself as a man of destiny, chosen to liberate his countrymen from their oppressors and usher in a new age of justice and prosperity. The fighting force he and Malick were going to build together, would be the means of accomplishing that sacred mission. He decided to call it the People's Redemption Army. PRA for short.

<><><><><>

In the same country where Kelli Kanekeh and Pablo Malick began to plan their insurgency, there is a village called George Town which lies about six miles to the east of the capital, Sewa City. It straggles the lower slopes of one of a semi-circle of thickly forested hills sheltering the city's south-eastern side.

Founded in the early nineteenth century, George Town was named after the king on the British throne at the time. Great Britain had taken over the running of the country and, having abolished the Slave Trade, the colonial government needed homes for Africans rescued from slave ships by the Royal Navy. All the villages established for this purpose were patterned after their English counterparts, with Anglican churches, vicarages and primary schools in one large compound. In the case of George Town, this former centre of community life had been built at the top end of the village, close to the edge of a forest reserve.

On the eastern boundary of the village, a stream still tumbles down the hill slopes all the year round, passing under the highway going up-country and onwards to the sea. It used to be the only source of fresh water when the village was established, and more than two hundred years later, continues to perform that service when the water taps run dry - an occurrence far too frequent for the liking of the village's inhabitants.

George Town's main road - Macaulay Street - goes right up the hill from the highway and ends in the open space in front of the Anglican compound. Like most of the streets in Sewa City, Macaulay Street was paved after the Second World War, but after several decades of being punished by torrential rains and the tyres of vehicles of every description, all that remains of its former smoothness are ragged patches of tar - like small islands in a dry river bed.

The first house on the left, immediately after the highway junction (No.2), belongs to an old widow called Mrs. Cobola Ennison. Everybody calls her 'Gramma Cobola'. Her house is a small clap-board bungalow set close to the road and surrounded by a bush-stick fence. She has tried to make her property a little more attractive by planting yellow/green croton bushes against the side of the fence facing the road. That side also accommodates her narrow gate and a rickety wooden stall where she sells matches, spools of black and white thread, pins and needles, cakes of local black soap, pieces of alum, various sweets and other small items. That is not all her merchandise, however. Gramma Cobola keeps the more expensive items indoors to thwart any dishonest and nimble-fingered visitors to her stall - things like batteries, tins of sardines, luncheon meat and corned beef.

On the same side of the street (No.4), Gramma Cobola's immediate neighbours used to be the Martins - Ola, Millicent and their only child, Emmanuel. *Their* house was set about six feet away from the edge of Macaulay Street, a more substantial building than Gramma Cobola's, since it had a large all-concrete room beneath the clap-board walls of the first floor. Ola Martin had built a store for wood and coal at the back of this room and a public bar at the front. He called the bar 'Millie's Corner' in honour of his wife.

It so happened that the very year in which Kelli Kanekeh embarked on his military campaign, Emmanuel Martin finally took his English teacher's advice and started recording some of the events of his life.

PART ONE

Chapter One

STORM WARNING

1 January 1993

New Year resolutions

1. Keep a diary to record my life and practise writing English.
2. Stop worrying about how I look.
3. Stop grumbling about housework.

10 January 1993

This is my first proper diary entry in spite of my New Year resolution. I shall try to do better; but I have to think of a good place to hide it in case Mams is tempted to find out if I have any secrets. I think under the mattress will be safe enough - on the other side near the wall.

Today is the sixth anniversary of Florrie's death. Mams wept a bit this morning and looked sad all day. As usual, she cooked beans in palm-oil and fried plantains and sent some for Gramma Cobola. Finger-licking delicious!!! Felt a bit guilty about enjoying the food so much when Mams had cooked it with a heavy heart and for a sad reason.

Lights tonight after three days without so I was able to study in comfort for my French test tomorrow.

3 February 1993

Big trouble. Caught smoking behind the toilets with 'the gang' during break. Jogolo sent us home with letters to the parents. One week suspension. One hard slap and a sharp-voiced lecture (Mams's punishment). Room arrest for one week (Dad's punishment). I'm only allowed to escape from these four walls to fetch water, eat and go to the toilet. The most annoying part is that I didn't even enjoy the thing. First it made me cough as if my throat would burst, then I felt dizzy the whole afternoon. Never again.

24 February 1993
Dad likes to say that people should always expect the unexpected. Today's events proved him right again. Foreigners have invaded the country - somewhere near the eastern border - hundreds of miles away from here, thank God! They say heavy fighting is going on and many of the border police have been killed. Soldiers have been sent up-country. When we were walking home from school, Khalid asked whether I was frightened. I said yes - at first - but not any more. Why? Because that part of the country is a long way away from here and anyway I'm sure our soldiers will deal with the invaders. After all, that is their job. They must be happy to have people to fight after being idle for all these years.

To Mass before school began because today is Ash Wednesday. Father Bassey made the usual ashes cross on our foreheads. Felt embarrassed about it for the first time and wiped it off as soon as I got outside. When Mams saw me again after school, she asked why I had done that and I told her the truth. She said, 'Manny, don't think because you are nearly fourteen you are too big to be humble before God.' But she didn't sound annoyed, only tired. And she had that line she gets between her eyebrows when she is upset. Thought it was because I wiped off the cross - that she was worried that I would grow up to be like Dad and refuse to go to church; but that wasn't the reason. Turned out that it was because of the invasion. She said she had a very, very bad feeling about it - the same feeling she had when Florrie got sick. She said she knew Florrie was going to die. Hmm. I am worried.

27 February 1993
Rendez-vous at the junction with Chico, Solade and Khalid this afternoon. We took turns trying out new stunts with Solade's new bicycle. <u>*Tres amusant*</u>. Only stopped when Chico in trying to avoid a car, fell in the gutter and scraped a lot of skin off his shin. Later Gramma Cobola came to say Modu had malaria so I had to help Dad in the bar. 'Millie's Corner' was packed full. Everybody is still talking about the invasion. Some people said they were not surprised it had happened because the government has allowed the country to become free for all. But they didn't seem at all worried. They even called for more beer and

stout than usual. Dad was pleased about the extra profit, but that did not stop him from shaking his head and telling me under his breath, 'These people are not serious. War breaks out and they are not even concerned.'

I said, 'Perhaps they are only pretending not to be concerned.'

Dad said, 'Perhaps,' but he didn't sound convinced.

10 March 1993

Gramma Cobola gave Khalid and me a lot of oranges when we passed her house after school. Her tree is loaded with oranges this year - the branches are weighed down. Modu is supposed to be sick again, but he was in the yard with her helping to count the ones she is going to sell. Whisky looked very much part of it all, lying beside Gramma Cobola, with his head on his paws, and thumping his tail when he saw us. Took Modu's place in 'Millie's Corner' again - reluctantly, because I had to rush through my history homework. Anyway, I scored. Dad allowed me to sample another of Mams's peppered fish before we opened. Finger-licking delicious!!! Begged for one more, but no luck this time.

I feel sorry for Mams, having to make peppered fish nearly every day. She must be so tired after teaching and going to market and cooking, yet the only thing she ever complains about is that her shoes don't last - unlike Dad who is always grumbling about the heat and dust in town and about how long he has to wait for transport. On the other hand, it must be very hard to work till 4 o'clock Monday to Friday, then struggle to get home, have a bath, sleep for one hour and open 'Millie's Corner' until 10 p.m. Really, my parents have a hard life. Mams says that is why I must try to do well in school - to make it all worthwhile for them. Doing my best, but I wish she hadn't told me that. She has put too much responsibility on my poor head.

The invasion is still the number one topic of conversation. People are now saying the invaders are not all foreigners; but no one seems to know who they are or why they have come to attack the country.

After school, Hamida ran up the hill to meet us just before we reached Gramma Cobola's market. Khalid scolded her for running -

playing big brother again - told her she would break her leg one of these days. Hamida just giggled - the same way Florrie used to giggle when I tickled her armpits. Ah, Florrie! The house has been so quiet since she left us.

18 April 1993

Fourteen years old today. My worst birthday so far. Woke up with a rash of new pimples all across my forehead, and no running water again. Down to the waterside four times this a.m. to fill buckets for baths and top up the drum. Good thing only the drum is upstairs otherwise I would have had to go up and down the back steps seven times in all. Why won't Dad change his mind about wards so *we* can have our own 'Modu' like Gramma Cobola? This work is becoming too much for me-oh.

Anyway, two good things happened today. Lights came back this evening after five weeks of blackout, and Dad and Mams gave me money for new shoes that don't have to conform with my school uniform. To 'CT Enterprises' this weekend to buy brown casuals like Khalid's.

30 April 1993

Special assembly for Forms Three to Upper Sixth this a.m. to listen to a talk by a Health Education Officer from the Ministry of Health - Mr. Yambasu. It was all about HIV/AIDS. The HEO got very angry because some boys laughed when he said we should be careful about using other people's blades and injections and about having sex. He said, 'You are laughing? If you people don't take what I am telling you seriously and use Durex when you want to play sex games with girls, your lives are going to be very short. This is a matter of life and death.'

Total silence till Pa Senevaratne asked whether mosquitoes could spread HIV. The HEO said no. Thank God for that, though I don't understand why. Mosquitoes take blood from one person to another just like blades and injection needles that are not clean. Wanted to tell the parents about the talk but embarrassed because of the sex part.

Noticed Gramma Cobola's flesh hanging like a thick fold of tripe when she raised her arm to fix her head tie - as if it is leaving her bones.

Very off-putting to see. Perhaps it's because she used to be so fat when she was young. She still asks us the same question every time we pass her house and greet her: 'Are you boys doing well and not disgracing your parents?' I wonder if she will ever realise that we are teasing her when we answer, 'Yes, Ma, no, Ma.'

She is a kind woman, though. Gave us both six black mints from her market.

Learned another French word for 'friend' today - *le copain.* We have decided to call ourselves that from now on - Chico, Solade, Khalid and Emmanuel. *Les copains.*

1 July 1993

One whole week without my voice making me feel stupid by cracking in the middle of a sentence. Praying that that embarrassment is almost over, leaving only pimples to cope with.

Up to Khalid's house to do maths homework together when rain ceased. As usual, road very nasty with red mud because of the downpour last night. No wonder Mams's shoes don't last - going up and down every day to school. Hard to believe the road used to be tarred all the way up to St. Stephen's compound. Dad says what can we expect in a village like ours when so many of the main roads in Sewa City are almost as bad. Very depressing.

So glad Khalid needs me to help him with English and French otherwise he might start feeling superior all round. At least, we are equal where school work is concerned. I scratch his back, he scratches mine. Hamida wanted to sit with us at the table, but Khalid drove her away - playing big brother again. He said, 'You talk too much. We won't concentrate.' I think Hamida was hurt, because she left the table without saying another word. But it's true. She always has something to say, that girl. And I wonder why her hair doesn't seem to grow. All the same, she's cute with her those big eyes of hers. Mama Abi gave me hot rice *Akara* when I went to say goodnight. Finger-licking delicious!!

Why do Whisky and his friends have to assemble right under my window every night to do their fighting and barking? I wish it would rain again - another downpour like the one we had last night, so they can get a good soaking.

20 September 1993

Military bulletins have started coming on the radio every day. Seems our soldiers are finding the rebels tough - that's what the Ministry of Defence is calling them now - 'rebels of the so-called People's Redemption Army.' They used to call them 'a bunch of thieves and bandits.' That must have been when they thought the army would defeat them easily. I wonder why the bulletins always refer to them as 'the enemy'. Perhaps it's easier to kill people when you don't think of them as human beings like yourself - just 'the enemy'. People are saying that many boys and young men up-country have joined the PRA. Hmm. Sounds bad. Mams looks worried most of the time but I think that is also because food is getting scarce - and more and more dear, she says.

Mammy B. heard Chico calling her 'Jaws' and reported him to Jogolo. After giving him a lecture about such rude behaviour, Jogolo told him Mammy B. has some sort of sickness and it's the medicine she has to take that is making her face look as if she stuffed tennis balls in her cheeks. Poor woman! Chico had to go and apologise to her. Felt guilty too, because we all call her 'Jaws'.

Where does sickness come from, I wonder. I can understand the ones like malaria and AIDS that are caused by germs and parasites, but these other strange things like what Mammy B has, and what killed Florrie. Why did Florrie's kidneys suddenly stop working when she was born healthy? Sometimes being alive is frightening! One day you are well, the next day you are sick, and if you are unlucky, you die before you grow up. In which case, what was the point of being born in the first place - just to suffer and make people sad?

30 October 1993

First class embarrassment today! Dad caught me in front of the parlour mirror inspecting my muscles. Instead of going away quietly, he stood there with his hands on his hips and a grin on his face. And to make matters worse, he said, 'Don't worry, Manny, they will show one of these days.'

He has no muscles - at least no muscles that show, which is what is worrying me - that I shall be like him and only have invisible muscles. Anyway, I know I am going to be taller because I can look straight into his eyes already - well almost. And if what Mams told me is true, I have seven more years to grow.

No lights again. Worried that my eyes won't last till I'm old, if things carry on like this. On the other hand, all those famous people like Shakespeare, Pythagoras, etc. did all that work before electricity was invented. Never heard that they went blind. All the same, I wish we had a lot of money like Pa Noah. Then we could buy our own generator and forget about NEC.

10 November 1993

To Confession after school. Only confessed about joining the others to call Mammy B. 'Jaws'. Penance was to say three extra decades on my rosary. I should have told Father Bassey about looking at the pictures Chico brought to school, but felt too ashamed. We took them to the toilet one by one during break. When I saw what the man and woman were doing, things happened and my pants grew so tight I was embarrassed even though I was alone. Had to stay there till things came back to normal. Afterwards we all laughed, but we avoided each other's eyes. Hmm. Mams would kill me if she knew!!! But I wonder what Dad would say. I'm sure he used to look at pictures like those ones when he was my age. I wish I could ask him, but too embarrassed.

Up to Khalid to do maths homework. When I arrived Pa Noah was on the veranda telling Alpha off for using his car as a taxi. Khalid said somebody saw the car loaded with people and reported to Pa Noah. As usual when he is angry, Pa Noah was speaking English. When he'd finished telling Alpha off, he shouted, 'Just get out of my sight, you scallywag.' Bit my lip to stop myself from laughing and didn't dare to look at Khalid. As for Alpha, I'm sure he'd never heard that word before, but from the way Pa Noah said it, he must have known it was an insult. He simply turned round and went down the steps. I think it's bye-bye Alpha. Couldn't help feeling sorry for him, with 2 wives and 8 children to support. Khalid was not at all sympathetic. He said Alpha should have thought of that when he was turning his boss's car into a taxi.' That is true, but still…

Why do these dogs have to bark so much? As soon as I think of a good way to do it, I'm going to deal with them.

14 November 1993

To early Mass with Mams. Lunchtime very enjoyable as usual. Beef stew with pigs' feet and Mams gave me the toes with thick gravy between them. Ginger beer too. I like it when the 3 of us eat together, but then if every day was like Sunday I wouldn't have Sunday to look forward to.

Mams announced that she is going to take her savings out of the post office because the value of her money keeps going down. She says she is going to start making bread rolls to sell to the small shops around here. Dad thinks it's a good idea, and said I should help with kneading the dough because that would make my muscles develop faster. Then he winked at me. I know he told Mams about catching me in the parlour because she said, 'Daddy, don't tease him.' Embarrassed. Anyway, I was happy when she added that I had enough to do already and she was going to hire a baker. Thank God!

Ironed all the clothes I washed yesterday. The coal was damp again, so the goose took one whole hour to get hot enough. It's that store! I think dampness enters from under the concrete floor. Very annoying. And the starch smelled sour - like stale *fufu.* Hope no one will notice it on my uniform and make embarrassing comments.

Played Ludo with Modu afterwards. It was a draw - 4/4. He told me that Mr. Danso's sister is a witch. Asked him how he knew that. As usual he said he heard somebody telling Gramma Cobola about something like that. I just sucked my teeth at him. Sometimes I wonder if that boy has any grey matter inside his head, the way he reports everything he hears as if it's the gospel truth.

19 November 1993

Jogolo was on the warpath because he caught boys smoking behind the toilets again - weed, this time. Hmm. None of *les copains* involved, thank God! He has threatened instant expulsion for anyone caught smoking marijuana again. He said, 'St. Peter's pupils should set a good example to boys from other schools. We have a tradition of excellence in every sphere going back more than one hundred years. You have a heritage to uphold. Don't you forget it.'

As from tomorrow, teachers are going to take turns patrolling the compound during break. Hmm. We'll have to mind our 'p's and q's', as Mammy B. would say.

Our backyard is still one big mess - clay everywhere, but the bread oven is almost complete. Looks like an upside down calabash big enough for someone to curl up inside. Mams says it's like some they have in Ghana. She's going to heat it with wood because that will be cheaper. The pantry is now full of racks and metal trays, all waiting for bread. A baker is coming from the Red Cross refugee camp at the old cement factory tomorrow 'to talk business.' Very excited. The only thing making me a bit miserable is that Mams says I shall have to help to supply her customers before going to school. When I said, 'That means I'll have to get up at least one hour earlier,' she said 'So?'

I hate it when she says 'So?' like that with her eyes wide open - as if I'm still a child she can bully. I have to start going to the waterside in the evenings as well.

25 November 1993

Mams has already found customers for her bread. Perhaps she and Dad will have more money to spare now. But at least they don't have to pay rent, for which Dad is always praising Grandpa (may his soul rest in peace). Dad says had his father been like some other men, he would have wasted all the money he made building for the British army during the Second World War on showing off, instead of buying land and building his own house. I'm happy that Uncle Eku gave his own half of the house to Dad in exchange for some other land. That means one day the house will be mine, unless the parents have another child. Somehow I don't think that will happen now. They have both started having grey hairs.

When the house is mine, I shall make it modern like Pa Noah's - with an inside kitchen, bathroom, flush toilet and a big water tank… No harm dreaming.

26 November 1993

The baker started work today. His name is Togbah Shepherd (Mams says I should call him 'Mr. Togbah' because he is a big man, even though he is a refugee).

I almost said 'Wow!!!' when I saw his muscles. He looks strong enough to lift a bag of rice in one sweep and walk a distance with it without sweating. If that is what kneading dough can do for a person, then Dad is right. Only one thing spoils his physique - his legs. They almost make an 'O' when he puts his feet together. Hard not to laugh at the way he walks, rocking from side to side.

First his country had a war and now we have a war. Hmm. What does it all mean?

1 December 1993

Learned another English word today - 'Pushover'. Mammy B. gave us this example: 'The PRA rebels are no pushover.' After last night's bulletin, no one had to open a dictionary to know what 'pushover' meant. Yesterday's battle was the bloodiest so far. The 'enemy' drove the government troops out of one town. The bulletin called it a 'tactical retreat.' I *have* to learn many more English words and expressions. I just love the language.

25 December 1993

Went to midnight Mass with Mams last night. For the first time sat with Solade at the back of the church instead of beside her. She wasn't pleased, but didn't insist. Today we ate the best cow-foot soup with salted pork and yam that Mams has ever made, but all in all, I think Christmas is over-rated.

26 December 1993

Boxing Day. Went to watch sports at the stadium with *les copains* wearing my Xmas present - blue polo shirt. Encountered several masquerading 'devils' along the way, but no incidents worth recording. Sports also quite boring except for the bicycle race.

28 December 1993

Whisky & co. got on my nerves too much with their non-stop barking and snarling. Decided to put my plan into action and threw the banger I had bought especially for them, out of the window and into their midst. They all leapt into the air with frightened yelps before scattering in all directions. Very, very funny. But now I feel a bit guilty. Why do I? They are only dogs, after all. Yet I can't stop feeling guilty. Can one 'sin' against animals? Anyway, they've moved away - never to return, I hope.

More war news. All bad. PRA rebels ambushed our soldiers again and killed many. Helicopters clattering overhead all day long, going to and from the military hospital.

Dad told us the church compound near his office is now full of people who have run away from the fighting up-country. He says the Red Cross officials call them IDPs, i.e. internally displaced persons. Most of the IDPs have only bundles and mats and they just sit there all day looking frightened and confused. Dad says he spoke to one man who told him that our soldiers are afraid of the rebels because they have brand new guns, and that if the government doesn't look out it will be bad for the whole country. Dad looked very worried while he was speaking and Mams said, 'What did I tell you? How can a country like this have an army worthy of the name when the lights in the *capital* are off more than they are on, and the water pipes are nearly always dry? Besides that, many of those army boys are thugs and school drop-outs. What do they know, and what do they care?'

Now *I* am getting scared. What if the fighting comes down here? And we *still* don't know what it is all about.

Chapter Two

RIPPLES ON THE WATER

1 January 1994

<u>New Year Resolutions</u>

1. Write in diary more often
2. Stop worrying about how I look
3. Stop grumbling about housework
4. Stop annoying Mams with my untidy room.
5. Read more English novels.

3 March 1994

Woke up with three big pimples on my left cheek and had to squeeze one because it was full of nasty pus! Felt so bad, I didn't want to go to school, but went all the same and toughed it out because I didn't want to miss 'Macbeth'. As expected, *les copains* teased me mercilessly, especially that Chico. Life is not at all fair. Why should he and Khalid not have pimples? Only Solade was sympathetic. He remembers what it was like for him last year. He advised me to rub Zambuk on my skin every night. Gramma Cobola doesn't sell it so had to go to the junction shop to buy some.

Today of all days Hamida was also there, buying an eraser. I don't think she noticed the pimples though, thank God! As usual, too busy talking - telling me all about 'Madame Meheux,' their new French teacher. She seems to have fallen for this Madame Meheux in a big way: Madame Meheux's skin is as smooth as a calabash and she looks like a doll. She has long hair like a mermaid and knows how to *dress.* She wears beautiful jewellery and talks as if she grew up in England, etc. etc. etc. Walked all the way up the hill with her afterwards. Khalid nowhere to be seen, so I didn't stay.

On the way back, saw Mr. Danso standing outside their family house. I admire the way his sister looks after him - clean shirt and trousers every time I see him and his hair nicely combed. Crossed the road and tried to keep my distance but he called out to me, asking for money to buy cigarettes. I laughed and said 'Mr Danso, where will a small boy like me get money? I'm not working yet.'

He said, 'Ask Millicent. She will give it to you.'

Amazed that he knew Mams and knew that I was her son. So he can't be as crazy as all that. When I told Mams she let out a big sigh and said, 'Poor fellow.... We grew up together, you know. He used to be so brilliant that he left all his classmates far behind. In those days, the principal of St Peter's was a white man - Mr. Hudson. He arranged for Danso to go to England to study medicine. That was where he went off his head.'

Hmm. Something else to worry about - going crazy.

10 April 1994

Another Monday over. During break, Solade announced that he is now 'born again' and no longer a Catholic. Next month he's going to be baptised again, he says - this time in a stream, because that is the proper way. Hmm.

Chico said, 'So long as you don't become too holy and start talking about Jesus all the time.' Annoyed and told him not to be flippant about Christianity. Chico reminds me so much of Dad. I know he'll stop going to church as soon as his parents leave him to decide for himself.

Had to help in 'Millie's Corner', but Dad released me after one hour because there were not many customers. This time it was Gramma Cobola who wasn't feeling well. She said pain from her 'atritis' was taking her to bed before her usual time so Modu would have to be inside the house quite early. She doesn't trust him enough to give him the key. Not surprised.

18 April 1994

My fifteenth birthday. Dad said my present is on its way. Hmm. I wonder what it is and why he couldn't buy it here. Mams presented me with Mum deodorant, saying 'Boys and girls your age need it.' That means my armpits have started offending her. How embarrassing! I'm glad she didn't tell me that to my face.

Nothing special to report from school, but a big tragedy when I went down to the petrol station to buy kero this evening. Mr. Deen's only son ran across the highway towards the petrol station to meet his father, and a Nissan taxi banged_him. Won't ever forget the sound of the collision. He died like a dog with his guts and blood spilling out. Everybody rushed to the spot, shouting, 'Lord have mercy-oh!!' Mr. Deen went crazy for several minutes. I even thought he was going to strangle the driver. But then he calmed down, took off his shirt and covered his son's body - so tenderly that everybody cried, even me, especially when he said, 'What have I been working for all these years - straining myself selling petrol till 11 o'clock every night just to be able to give the boy a good education?' Very, very sad. Had to buy two pints of kero from a street seller, instead of being able to fill up the container at the petrol station.

22 April 1994

Terrible, terrible news from the warfront. The worst so far. PRA have overrun the main diamond fields around Dembu. Many government soldiers killed. Hmm. Asked Mr. Togbah about the war in his country, but he didn't seem to want to talk about it. All he said was, 'My young friend, war is a very bad thing. Just keep praying that the fighting does not reach us down here.'

He sighed loudly, shaking his head over and over again as if even after four years, all the bad experiences he had in his own country are still too fresh in his mind. He says that when he ran away the only things he was able to bring with him were the clothes on his back, the small bit of money he had in his pocket and his cassette/radio. He brings it to work every day and plays the same tape all the time because it is the only one he has. Bob Marley. Didn't like the reggae beat at first, but he said, 'My young friend, forget about the beat and listen to the words. The man was like a prophet.'

Now I know what he means. My favourites are 'One Love', 'Redemption Song', 'Don't you worry about a thing.' Mr. Togbah calls Bob Marley 'a shooting star' because he died at a very early age. I have to admit that I even like the reggae beat now, though I still don't find it as exciting as *soukous.* Give me Papa Wemba and Kanda Bongo Man any day. Those Congolese people know how to make guitars *siiing-oh.* I feel the music *inside* my heart.

Feeling extra tired tonight. Perhaps I did too much kneading - four big lumps of dough. But IT IS WORKING - muscles definitely getting bigger and harder.

4 May 1994

Wonderful surprises today - parcels from Uncle Eku, brought from America by one of his friends. Got a Nokia calculator (from him) and Levi Strauss jeans - my birthday present from Dad. The jeans are a bit long but otherwise perfect - Dad must have given Uncle Eku my measurements. God bless them both!

First class embarrassment later when I was helping Dad to clean up in 'Millie's Corner' before opening time. Out of the blue he said, 'Manny, when I was your age, we used to share information about everything, and I am sure it is the same with you and your gang; but your mother says I should talk to you about sex...By the way, I hope you have not started doing it yet.'

Not knowing where to put my eyes, I answered truthfully, 'No, sir.'

He said, 'Good. There's plenty of time for that. But you think about girls and about doing it, don't you?'

I could hardly get the words out but again, told him the truth.

'Yes, sometimes.'

The next question was even *more* embarrassing. Had I noticed any strange marks on my bed sheet? Before I could answer that one, he said, 'It's nothing to be ashamed of, you know. It only means that you are becoming a man. Anyway, your mother wants me to tell you about two things in particular.'

One, the sicknesses that a person can catch through having sex, especially this terrible new one called HIV/AIDS - had I heard about them? When I said yes, I had to tell him what I knew. Was amused when he said, 'Excellent' after I described the HEO's visit. He sounded just like Pa Senevaratne. The next thing was that he and Mams didn't want any parent or guardian coming to No.4 Macaulay Street to say I had made their daughter or ward pregnant - was that clear?

In short, I am to behave in a responsible way and respect girls, and I *must* use Durex when I start 'doing it'.

Most embarrassing moments of my life so far. Probably embarrassing for Dad too, but he didn't show it. I think I have good parents. But they give me too much work.

4 June 1994

Bread delivery as usual, then laundry, then to Sewa City with Khalid to buy an airmail to write and thank Uncle Eku for the calculator. Khalid admired my muscles which pleased me no end though I played it cool. Dad is sure to notice them soon, if he hasn't already done so, and he's bound to say something embarrassing. Determined to play it cool again.

Khalid treated me to a haircut at 'Hot Looks'. Very pleased with my 'fade' but didn't like the rap music blasting all the time. Give me my *soukous* any day - even Bob Marley. Strolled back home giving some of the girls we saw marks out of ten. Only two got eight, the rest got six and below. Just before Macaulay Street junction we saw ten military lorries heading up-country one after the other, *loaded.* They moved and sounded like old elephants with rheumatic pain - reminded me of Gramma Cobola. Khalid said they didn't look as if they would reach the war front and I agreed. It is still hundreds of miles away, thank God!!

Mams was annoyed because I got home after 2 p.m. and said I would have to help Mr. Togbah instead of going back to the junction for a rendez-vous with *les copains.* She doesn't like my new haircut either; said, 'Just fade away from my sight,' when I told her what the style is called, then, 'I am surprised Mr Aki-Crowther allows you boys to go to school looking like that.'

She'll soon get used to it. She has to.

I was annoyed too - about not being allowed to meet *les copains.* Took off my shirt and punished dough till I was covered with sweat. Mr. Togbah made me wrap a towel round my body so the sweat wouldn't drip. Still annoyed, I asked who would know if my sweat fell into the dough and he said, 'My young friend, that is not the point. You should always try to do the right thing, even when no one will know. And don't forget that God is always watching.' Hmm.

Mr. Togbah made me feel ashamed of myself for not caring about sweat in the dough so I made a confession later. My penance was an extra 'Hail Mary'. I wonder how Father Bassey feels, listening to some of our rubbishy confessions. I'm sure they make him laugh sometimes - or feel like laughing.

15 June 1994

Just as I thought! When I went to say goodbye to Papa before going to Mass, he looked, he grinned, then he said, 'Hmm. The muscles are coming on, eh.'

As planned, I grinned back at him and said, 'It's kneading dough. You were right.' He tilted his head as if to say, 'You see?' End of story.

History and Geography exams tomorrow. Revised for 2 hours after lunch, then Khalid came down. He fell for Melrose Amara at Intersec. Sports and wanted me to help him compose a letter to her. Can't see what he likes about her, with those thin legs, but each to his own taste.

Final version of the letter kept for future reference:

'I have been observing you for several weeks now and have to tell you that I have fallen for your exceptional beauty, especially those large brown eyes and well shaped, kissable lips.
Please be my girl friend. You will not regret it '

We took a long time deciding how to end the letter and finally wrote *'Hopefully yours,'* because it sounded clever.

I'm sure Melrose will accept him - tall, no pimples, well-built, plenty of money... No, I *don't* envy Khalid, though it would be good if the parents had more cash to spare - and if I didn't have pimples.

1 July 1994

Experienced the worst storm last night - almost what I imagine a hurricane would be like - wind howling, rain roaring; trees and other heavy objects crashing all around the place. It lasted for more than one hour. Very, very frightening. Part of the Noahs' roof flew down the hill and landed on top of the Dansos' house. Maybe that is what saved their roof. So many people lost their roofs; but *we* were lucky - well, according to Dad, it wasn't a matter of luck. He looked and sounded quietly satisfied when he said, 'Manny, these old wooden houses are much stronger than they look. Nowadays the contractors are only interested in their profit. Where they should put ten nails, they put in four.'

Ever since daybreak people have been rushing around trying to fix their roofs before the next downpour, so we heard nothing but bang, bang, bang all day long. Carpenters and people who sell CI roofing sheets must be delighted with all the profit they have made today. Many electric wires were brought down by uprooted trees, so even if it is our turn to have lights, we won't. Our bad luck.

24 November 1994

I hope Solade isn't turning into a religious fanatic. The discussion we had today points that way. He said only born-again Christians will go to heaven, and also that among Christians, Catholics will be the first to be excluded from heaven because we believe things that are not in the Bible - things like Purgatory, and praying to saints. I wasn't in the arguing mood, but Khalid challenged him straightaway, asking whether he meant that all Muslims would go to hell even if they had tried to live good lives according to the Koran. Without any hesitation, Solade said, 'Yes. Only people who believe the Bible is the word of God and take Jesus as their personal saviour will go to heaven.'

Chico said, 'But what about people who don't know anything about the Bible, and have never heard about Jesus Christ? What about them, hmm?'

Solade said he didn't know about them. He was only going by what was in the Bible.

'That doesn't make sense,' Chico said flatly.

'And who says your Bible is the only word of God,' Khalid added. 'There is only one God. Allah Himself gave the Koran to Mohammed (Peace be unto Him), and he was the last messenger.'

At that point Solade declared Islam to be a false religion which so enraged Khalid that the veins in his neck stood out like cords. He shouted, 'What! What did you say? What did you say? You are lucky that you live in a country like this. In some other places they would slit your throat for saying something like that.'

'It won't matter,' Chico said with an annoying laugh. 'He will go straight to heaven.'

Solade just walked away which made Khalid turn on Chico, saying it was wrong to ridicule people's religious beliefs; to which he replied, 'Even if they are ridiculous?'

I said, 'Yes, because that is only *your* opinion.'

Chico's lips clamped shut as if he wanted to continue arguing but decided against it. Solade kept away from us for the rest of the afternoon, but we'll be friends again tomorrow. That is what always happens.

As for religion, I wonder if Solade is right and I shouldn't call myself a Christian, even though I believe in God and Jesus Christ. What I find hard to believe is that people who follow other religions sincerely will end up in hell. Also, who is to say one holy book is truer than another? And in any case, would a just and loving God sentence good, kind people to eternal roasting because they are not Christians? It's like that old reggae record they still play on the radio - 'There are more questions than answers...'

To bed to rest my weary brain. I wonder whether too much thinking is what makes some people go crazy.

1 December 1994

Tried to persuade Dad to buy new cassettes for 'Millie's Corner' because I am tired of Jim Reeves, Don Williams and Kenny Rogers all the time. He said nobody had complained except me, which means I don't count. Never mind Emmanuel, no condition is permanent. One fine day, you'll be able to do what you want.

Chapter Three

RISING WIND

1 January 1995

<u>New Year Resolutions</u>

1. Write in diary more often
2. Stop worrying about how I look
2. Be more cheerful over housework
3. Start 'O' level revision on February 1
4. Stop kicking my dirty clothes under the bed

2 March 1995

Making New Year resolutions is a complete waste of time. Apart from starting 'O' level revision, I have broken all of them already. No more after this year.

Lights out again - second day. Dozed off while studying last night. Somehow my hand touched the candle flame and my skin started to burn - fortunately - because the pain woke me up. The parents came running when they heard me shout and Mams exploded though surprisingly, not at me for being careless. She shouted, 'Those bastards!! Forcing our children to use candles to study in this day and age. And *they* all have generators. I hope they roast in hell!!'

I never thought I would hear Mams using rough language. Not after the way she scrubbed my tongue and teeth with Lifebuoy soap when she heard me say 'bastard' when I was ten, and the reproachful looks she gives Dad when *he* lets go in front of her. She must have been really upset on my behalf - and also frightened at the thought of what could have happened to this old house. My hand is not badly burned, thank God!!

18 April 1995

My sixteenth birthday. Got some money from Dad, but I haven't yet decided what to buy - perhaps new underpants or a singlet or novels from the 'Bend-down Bookshop' on the pavement to enjoy after 'O' levels. That is if I can find some clean ones. Black socks from Mams -

boring, but appreciated because my big toes and heels are showing through the old ones.

Jogolo on the warpath. He lectured the whole school for fifteen minutes about our 'comportment' - no shirts outside trousers when in uniform (guilty), no raised voices or general rowdiness in the street (not guilty), no bad language (not guilty in public) - all because some Form Three boys got into a fight and the news reached him.

This time he said, 'Boys from St. Peter's should always behave like gentlemen. If you want to be a hooligan, this is not the place for you. Find another school. Do I make myself clear?' Total silence as we went back to class. But of course, it didn't last.

Helicopters whirring overhead while we were walking home from school. Chico asked the question which must be on everybody's mind these days. It had certainly been in mine.

'Suppose this war gets so bad they start forcing young people to join the army?'

Khalid said, 'Allah forbid! The people who are paid to defend the country should do their job.'

To which we all heartily agreed. Imagine having to go to the bush to fight!

Hamida arrived at Macaulay Street junction just as Khalid and I were turning in and we walked up the hill together. She is becoming tall - head above my shoulder. And she doesn't talk so much these days. When I made a remark about it, she said in a very cool voice, and putting on her best Madame Meheux accent, 'This is the new me.'

To which I replied, 'I liked you better the way you used to be.'

'That's too bad,' she said.

I wanted to cut her down to size but couldn't think of a clever reply, so I said, 'And you are becoming very cheeky, too,' which made her give me one cold look and quicken her steps.

'Don't mind her,' Khalid said as she moved ahead of us. 'That's how she behaves at home nowadays.'

I wonder what it's all about. Maybe she's suffering from growing pains.

Another storm starting. To bed to enjoy the sound of rain on the roof.

25 April 1995
A red letter day. Military music was playing when Dad switched on the radio for the news this morning. He shouted to Mams and me to come and listen, saying he thought there'd been a coup.

It was indeed a coup. When the music stopped, an officer came on the air. He sounded young and out of breath and very angry. He said a Military Revolutionary Council had taken over the government because they were fed up with the rubbish going on in the country. The government sent them to fight a war with guns that were always overheating and refusing to fire, and with vehicles that were always breaking down and running out of petrol. Also, they didn't have good communication equipment and they had to be able to communicate fast because the PRA use guerrilla tactics. On top of all that, the food they were getting was unfit even for jailbirds; and they had not been paid for three months. He said they had complained and complained but the Ministry of Defense had turned deaf ears, so they had been forced to act. He appealed to everyone to stay calm and to carry on business as usual and asked God to bless us all.

Dad's reaction was, 'Well, well, well! but mind you, I'm not at all surprised after the way things have been going.'

Just as Mams was wondering aloud what had become of the president and his cabinet, Gramma Cobola called from the bottom of the back steps to find out whether we had heard the news. When I said yes, she went back to her house, complaining loudly about her aching bones though the pain wasn't bad enough to make her forget to remind me to try hard and not disgrace my parents.

There were soldiers everywhere on the way to school. They looked so rough and cocky that Khalid and I kept our distance. With so much tension in the air, it was hard to concentrate on lessons. When Dad came home from work, he told us the president and all the cabinet had fled by helicopter, but no one knows where to as yet.

I said, 'If the rebels are fighting to overthrow the government and the government has been overthrown, the war should be over.'

Dad said, 'Good point.' but Mams grunted in a doubtful way and said that she still had a very bad feeling about the whole thing.

Dad said, 'Millie, you and your bad feelings,' and changed the subject. He doesn't like it when people talk about visions and prophecies and bad feelings. He says that sort of thing is all superstition and is what has made Africa the dark continent to this day.

30 April 1995

Another unforgettable day. As if the rebels heard what I said about there being no reason for the war to continue, a Colonel Cobra, 'spokesman for the PRA' came on the BBC this evening (*Focus on Africa*) when Dad and I were tidying up at 'Millie's Corner'. The presenter said he was using a satellite phone - whatever that is. Colonel Cobra said that what was going on in the country was in fact a revolution and it would not be over until everyone connected with the old government had gone. He said the PRA had to continue fighting because not only the corrupt government had to go by force. Its army and its police had to go as well because *they* were the government's watchdogs.

'And they are all corrupt,' he declared with contempt. 'All of them. If they remain, the lives of the suffering masses of this country will never improve. This country is sick - even dying. We of the PRA are fighting to save it. So, as the late Samora Machel used to say, 'the struggle continues.'

Very impressed by Colonel Cobra's speech even though he pronounced 'country' 'cowntry' and his voice sounded as hoarse as if he spends every day shouting like a sergeant-major or sitting in a kitchen full of smoke. We definitely need a change. However, Dad looked gloomy when he had finished.

'Manny, mark my words,' he said. 'Very soon this country is going to become like Congo in 1960 or like Angola…complete and utter chaos.'

'But Dad, how else will things ever change?' I asked, since I consider myself one of the suffering masses.

'Am I to take it that you support this war?' Dad replied.

I had never heard him sound so cold, which should have warned me that I was treading on dangerous ground. Instead of heeding the warning, like a fool, Emmanuel answered, 'In a way. Dad, you yourself have said that elections in this country are a sick joke. And now we even have a military government.'

'So you think war is the way to solve those problems,' he remarked.

I didn't reply because his voice was now making me feel as if he was pouring ice water down my back. He went on, 'I can't believe a Form Five boy at St. Peter's has become a rebel supporter on the strength of what a 'spokesman' said. How do you know this Colonel Cobra is sincere? How do you know the PRA are any better than the ones they are trying to remove?'

I now felt about two feet tall, and he hadn't finished with me yet.

'No one can deny that this country is in trouble. But from what I have seen and heard, I know that war is not the answer. What is happening up-country is making matters worse. The government no longer controls the diamonds, when selling diamonds overseas is what brings imported things into the country; and the fighting is making more and more people unable to work. Haven't you heard that farmers are abandoning their farms because of the fighting and that so many schools and health centres have been burnt down? The little that previous governments did for the country and what we inherited from the British is all being wrecked and the cost of living is going up every day - ask your mother. *I* will never, ever support a war, Emmanuel, and no intelligent person should. I am only excusing you because you are still a small boy.'

Two feet tall? I felt like a cockroach - only fit to be squashed. Apart from asking me to do this and that in the same cold voice, he didn't speak to me for the rest of the evening.

I understand his point of view, but still think that war is sometimes necessary. Anyway, I hope our quarrel blows over by tomorrow. I hate tension as much as I hate embarrassment.

1 May 1995

Told *les copains* about the bust-up with Dad. They agreed with me, though Solade said people should only support war if they are prepared to go and fight or to send their own children to fight; otherwise they are being hypocrites. He has a point. I certainly don't want to interrupt my studies to go to the bush to fight and perhaps even cut my life short.

5 May 1995

Full moon. As usual Mr.Danso is singing hymns at the top of his croaky voice. Tonight it is '*Nearer my God to Thee*'- all the verses, I think. Holy Mary mother of God, please keep craziness far from me! I think it's better to be dead than permanently crazy.

No more diary till 'O' levels are over. English Literature tomorrow. Mams surprised me with a cup of Milo to make me sleep well. Too tired to study, anymore. What will be will be. Dad and I are on good terms again, thank God!!

20 June 1995

Don't know how I survived the last two weeks. I think I did well, though I'm not sure about Geography and Maths. Anyway, that is over. Tonight I shall sleep like a well-fed baby.

30 June 1995

Up to Khalid's house to watch video. Saw an old film called 'The Getaway'. It was so exciting that I was on the edge of my seat the whole time. Normally Hamida would have been shouting like us, but she was as quiet as ever. I am beginning to feel a bit uncomfortable around her.

19 July 1995 (written after Mass on 20 July)

To Confession, though no sin to report, except that I grumbled to myself when I had to stand in for Modu again last Saturday. I don't think that counts because God knows how much I wanted to go to see '*The School Inspector*' at the British Council with *les copains.*

To Chico's house later for our school leaving party. Food was finger-licking delicious, including Mams's peppered fish, and *sweet* music, most of it chosen by me. Solade calls it 'Satan's music' now and says dancing is sinful, so he didn't come to the party. He doesn't know what he missed!! Wore my Levi Strauss jeans and blue and white striped shirt bought with Dad's birthday money. Rolled up the sleeves to display my muscles. Knew I looked good, which gave me confidence to chat up Belinda Adams. She looked so sexy in her black jeans that I wanted to hold her straightaway. I danced with her most of the evening and she let me hold her close when Lionel Ritchie was singing 'You're my lady.' Things started happening so I had to put more distance between us. Very embarrassing. I hope she didn't notice. I want to send her that letter though Chico says he has seen her twice in a big man's car. So? He could be her uncle.

It started to rain heavily just before we reached home and I got soaked to the skin, but felt on top of the world.

20 July 1995 (written before going to bed)

A very ordinary Sunday. To Mass with Mams. Nice lunch as usual. Tired after last night so I spent part of the afternoon in bed reading *Rage of Angels,* the Sidney Sheldon I borrowed from Chico. It was almost as exciting as watching a video. Later Dad invited me to play draughts and beat me hands down. He is more cheerful these days; told me that he looks forward to getting out of bed because things seem to be improving since the MRC took over. Don't know how they have managed it, but lights almost every other day now and they have even started clearing the mountains of garbage and repairing the roads in Sewa City. Dad says perhaps the country is going to join the twentieth century at last. Even the warfront seems quiet.

26 July 1995

'Rain, rain, rain, will you never stop. I am getting tired of your plop, plop, plop.'

Mams says she doesn't remember a rainy season as wet as this one. At this rate we'll soon run out of clean clothes because everything is damp and beginning to smell bad. Bored out of my skull, especially since I have no more home-work for the time being. Not our turn to have electricity and when it's raining, this house is too dark to read without lights on. Haven't seen Khalid and Hamida for four days now. Will go up there tomorrow no matter what. At least there we can watch a video.

Still thinking about Belinda Adams. Can't decide if I should try to 'raid' her or forget her. Was she really interested or just flirting with me?

27 July 1995

Rain lessened for a while this p.m. Up to the Noahs as I had promised myself. Watched Sylvester Stallone film, 'The Specialist'. Very, very exciting but there were too many big explosions. I have come to the conclusion that I don't like so much violence. Hamida was her usual quiet self, but she asked about the party. She and Khalid are going to London next week to stay with Mama Abi's younger sister. Lucky them.

Mr. Togbah was in a talkative mood when we were making bread today. One story after the other about when he used to be a sailor. He has been round the world - Abidjan, Takoradi, Tema, Lagos, Douala, Cape Town, Pointe Noire, Hong Kong, Kuala Lumpur, Liverpool, New York...etc. etc. etc. I love the names of those places. And says he has fourteen children from women in six countries!! But he says the work was too hard and he always had to bribe agents at the port to be put on a ship, so he got fed-up. I hope I will be able to travel and see foreign countries one day. Nowadays people are afraid to travel even in this country.

2 August 1995

Fell asleep early last night then woke with a start because of the angry voice I heard coming from the parents'room. I tiptoed to their door and listened outside. My heart jumped when I heard Mams say, 'Ola, I can never forgive you for this. Never.'

She sounded as if she had been crying. Dad said something in reply, but couldn't make it out. I crept back to bed feeling very nervous and didn't really sleep again until daybreak. Noticed that the parents didn't say one word to each other this morning. I asked Mams what was wrong. She said, 'Ask your father.' Asked Dad the same question. He said 'Manny, life is complicated. Let's leave it at that for now.' So I'm none the wiser and feeling even more nervous - the same way I felt when Florrie got sick.

4 August 1995

Gramma Cobola called me this morning when Mams went to market to ask how things were at home. She had a certain look in her eyes, so Mams must have told her about the quarrel. Unfortunately, I had no information to give her.

I asked Mr. Togbah's advice about what to do and he told me to mind my own business. But it *is* my business. They are my parents and I live here.

No peppered chicken prepared for 'Millie's Corner' since August 2. So this thing is really, really serious!

Decided to send that letter to Belinda via Chico, with slight changes. Hope she agrees to become my girlfriend. For one thing, while Khalid is away, it will give me somewhere to go to escape from the atmosphere here. This place is like a house where someone just died.

10 August 1995

Chico brought my reply from Belinda. 'Come to my house this afternoon and I shall give you my answer.'

I went, feeling a little bit timid. She has agreed to be my girlfriend, but the visit was not all that wonderful. a) because conversation did not flow. b) because I don't think her mother likes me. Anyway, I'm going back to visit her on Saturday. Hmm. Not so sure now.

Is this new water pipe they started laying ever going to reach George Town? Had to go to the waterside again early this morning because there wasn't enough water left over for Dad's bath. Downstream, there were some women, all dressed in white, praying at the top of their voices with lighted candles all around them. One of the women was waving a dead white chicken above her head as she prayed. Noticed a naked girl in their midst. When I went back the second time, they had just left. A little boy in shirt-tails came and pounced on the candles as if he had been hiding in the bushes, waiting for the women to go. Our eyes met and he scampered over the rocks like a dog that had just stolen a piece of meat. *Tres amusant.*

20 August 1995
Lights on this p.m. so I was able to finish my Wilbur Smith *River God.* The book has taken me back five thousand years to live in ancient Egypt - right away from the tension in this house. A wonderful experience!

24 August 1995
I can't get used to not having lunch with the parents on a Sunday. Straight after Mass, Mams said she was going out - she never goes out on a Sunday. Dad asked me to help him paint 'Millie's Corner'. It turned out that he wanted to tell me what their quarrel is about.

One light push could have knocked me to the ground when he said, 'Manny, I won't beat about the bush. I have another child. She's called Melvina and she is six years old.' My legs felt as weak as they did the first time I drank cider, and they still don't feel normal.

Dad said it happened after Florrie died and Mams was always crying and did not want to have any 'relations' with him. S*oooooo* embarrassed when I realized what he was talking about - ten times more than when he talked to me about 'doing it' with Durex'. I felt like putting my hands over my ears so I wouldn't hear more.

Apparently, he never told Mams about Melvina's existence. Now the mother is emigrating and begged Dad to take Melvina for a while because all her close family live abroad except her mother, and *she* is old. Before he could give her an answer, Dad had to confess to Mams. Mams became very upset - who would blame her? And she has said, 'no way' about having Melvina in our house.

Dad said, 'Manny, I understand how your mother feels, but I wish she too would understand what happened. I needed somebody to hold me after we buried Florrie. She was my little angel.'

His voice cracked as if he was about to start crying, which would have been too much for me to take. I quickly said, 'But Dad, why did you keep quiet about it for all these years?'

He sighed before replying, 'Manny, you still have a lot to learn. In time to come, you will find out that words can be too heavy to say sometimes. I can't tell you how many times I began to tell your mother and then lost courage. But the thing is, Melvina is here and she is my daughter. I can't disown her.'

I didn't know what to say after that, so I just carried on painting till we finished. What a mess!! In a way; I sympathize with him, but at the same time feel angry that he exposed his weakness to me, his son, and that he has upset Mams so much. I don't think children should know everything about their parents. Too embarrassing even to think of him 'doing it, and now I have a sister I knew nothing about, Mams feels betrayed and the house has that funeral atmosphere again.

Enough for one day. Let me go to bed.

25 August 1995

Mams says my face always shows it when there is something on my mind, so I wasn't surprised when, as soon as she saw me this morning, she muttered, 'He's told you, eh?'

After Dad went to work, we talked. She is as immoveable as a rock about not having Melvina here. Not that she has anything against the child, she says, but she can't forgive Dad for going to another woman at a time when he knew she was in such pain, then hiding the result from her all these years and now expecting her 'to take his out-of-wedlock child.'.

She says Melvina will just have to go to her grandmother. I can't help feeling very sorry for the child even though I have never seen her face. It's not her fault.

1 September 1995

Khalid and Hamida came back from London today. Felt very happy to see them again. Both of them brought me presents. Khalid, a black leather wallet and Hamida, a ballpoint pen that changes the colour of the ink when you turn the barrel round. Very touched that they thought of me, especially Hamida who has been so strange lately. As she handed the pen to me, I noticed for the first time how clear the whites of her eyes are - like the inside of eggshells.

Khalid walked part of the way home with me and said, 'My c*opain*, what's up? You don't seem like your usual self.'

I told him about the problem with the parents and he asked whether I thought they would make it up. I don't know. That's what is so upsetting. I hate having to talk to them separately all the time.

Anyway, Khalid has brought some new videos. Something else to take me away from my own war zone from time to time.

15 September 1995

To St. Peters to register for Form Six. I find it very strange to be in a class with eighteen people instead of thirty. Only six of us are doing the same subjects. Solade and Khalid are prefects. I have been nominated Head Boy. Wow!

Went to town with *les copains* after registration to buy khaki for long trousers. Took material to the tailor, feeling *really* proud of myself.

Thinking about getting to know my newly revealed sister, but don't feel ready to do so yet. Still too upset and confused. Saw a few hairs on my chin for the first time when I was combing my hair. Hmm. That means I'll have to start shaving soon.

16 September 1995

'O' level results any day now. My heart misses a beat whenever I think about it. What with tension in the house and tension in my head, just had to escape this afternoon. Went first to Belinda. Conversation still dry. She only likes reading Mills and Boon love stories and she doesn't like action films, only those miniseries like 'A woman of substance', with a lot of love and passion. She likes to play Ludo, but finds Scrabble and cards boring. So we just sat together and held hands after she had told me that her parents are divorced. But she turned my head to her and kissed me quickly, even though her two younger sisters were sitting on the other side of the veranda. That made it all the more exciting. What I like most about Belinda is that she doesn't pretend to be shy. Perhaps our conversations will improve when we know each other better.

To the Noahs later. Watched a great film called 'The Bodyguard' - action, suspense and a bit of romance - just what I like + Whitney Houston singing. Noticed Hamida wiping tears from her cheeks when Rachel (Whitney) and Frank (forgotten his real name) kissed passionately at the end and also when Rachel sang 'I will always love you.' When Khalid teased her about it, she got up and walked away. The girl is becoming too strange for my liking.

Dogs yapping non-stop as I ran down the hill to our house. Picked up some stones just in case they attacked me; but they kept their distance. I think the word has gone round that that person they call Manny is a wicked human being.

20 September 1995

'O' level results came out today. Grade One with two ones (English and Economics), two twos (French and History). Credits in Biology, Geography, Chemistry and - I passed Maths. Better than I expected, thank God!

Dad gave me a tight hug and said 'Good boy!!' Mams gave me a peck right on my lips and said, 'Glory be to Jesus! I am so proud of you, Manny. Proud and very happy.'

And she looked much happier than she had done for a long time. She was smiling and her forehead was as smooth as Mr Togbah's best loaves. They both asked me what present I wanted - but separately, which lowered my spirits again. Anyway, I am expecting a good watch from Dad and a Walkman from Mams. And she is going to start paying me something for helping Mr. Togbah. All in all, worth straining my eyes for. Felt on top of the world, especially when Jogolo looked at us over his glasses and said, 'You boys have done St. Peters proud. Well done!'

All *les copains* did well, especially Solade - eight distinctions - all ones!! As expected, when we congratulated him he said, 'Jesus really worked for me!!', to which Chico replied, 'Don't tell me that. It was all your own effort. You studied day and night.'

Solade just smiled in that irritating way he does sometimes - as if he knows something *we* don't know. I wonder whether I would have done better if *I* were born again. Too late now. Anyway, I'm satisfied with my results. Doing my three best subjects for 'A' levels - English, Economics and French.

22 September 1995

Rendez-vous at the junction with *les copains*. We sat on the wall by the highway munching boiled groundnuts, bossing and watching the world go by. We were forced to remember the war when a military lorry broke down near the junction. The officer in charge got very annoyed when he saw us laughing, and said, 'Left to me, idle boys like you would be at the war front. That will teach you to laugh when people who are fighting for you find themselves in difficulty.'

We hadn't been laughing at their plight, but we nonetheless wiped the grins from our faces and even offered to find a mechanic for them. I went to call Toyota Barrie from across the highway. Turned out to be a minor problem with the gearbox. As the soldiers drove away, Toyota Barrie passed on the news that the officer had told him that by this time next month the war will be over except for 'mopping up operations'.

I'll believe that when we stop seeing IDPs heading towards Sewa City with their bundles.

30 September 1995

Dad says he has heard that some white mercenaries called 'Security Solutions' are now in the country and are going to help the MRC government to deal with the rebels. They have helicopter gunships. Wow! No wonder that officer said the war would soon be over.

5 November 1995

Looks as if the PRA are really finished. War bulletin this evening said 'Security Solutions' have driven them out of the Dembu area after fierce fighting. The PRA suffered heavy, heavy losses and those who escaped have fled deep into the forest. Can't help feeling a bit disappointed that the excitement is coming to an end. Thank goodness Dad can't read my mind. He would disown me if he knew.

Chapter Four

THE PRA LICKS ITS WOUNDS

Giant trees formed a dense green canopy which completely concealed Camp Freedom where Kelli Kanekeh, leader of the People's Redemption Army, was pacing the uneven, earthen floor of his quarters like a caged leopard. He was deep in thought - so much so that he did not realize how tightly his jaw and fists were clenched. In the past year, the war to liberate the country suddenly started going wrong, cancelling out months of steady progress which had won them the diamond fields and had begun to fill Malick's pockets nicely. For some reason, after the coup, the government troops had begun to fight with more determination. Then to make matters worse, the new gang of thieves and rogues in the capital had shown that they had no more national pride than the previous gang. What they did when they saw that the PRA fighters were overcoming their own forces was unforgivable - absolutely unforgivable - hiring white mercenaries - the lowest of the low, to kill their own brothers and sisters - sons and daughters of the soil. For the promise of diamond concessions, no doubt. In the heat of his anger, Kanekeh gathered saliva and spat on the ground with the force of a slap.

During the battle for the diamond fields, the dirty-dog mercenaries had pursued his fighters with helicopter gunships, firing missiles that within minutes had reduced the bodies of his bravest boys to bloody scraps of flesh and bone. The rest of his fighters had had to scramble for cover like chickens fleeing hawks. An unbearable humiliation after months of triumph.

Kanekeh continued to pace up and down for a few minutes longer, then with sudden resolve, wheeled round, strode out to the entrance of the hut and bellowed, 'Colonel Cobra,' in the commanding tone he had adopted since assuming leadership of the PRA. It demanded and received instant obedience, so it was hardly surprising that, on hearing his leader's summons, the young man addressed as 'Cobra,' sprang to his feet at once.

He had been sitting under the overhanging branches of a massive flamboyant tree ablaze with its scarlet flowers, playing a fierce game of draughts with another commander they called 'Leopard.' Cobra's sudden movement overturned the crudely made draught board, sending the counters flying in all directions; but instead of expressing annoyance, Leopard muttered, 'Thank God,' a sentiment echoed by the other commanders who had been watching the game. *They* also leapt to their feet though only Cobra had been summoned.

Their leader had not left his quarters for days, not even to perform the daily exercises about which he was such a fanatic. In fact, the only sign that he was still alive were the bowls of food and water his woman took inside every morning and evening. Not knowing what plans he had for the PRA after that crushing defeat, their morale had plummeted.

Hastily doing up the buttons of his shirt, Cobra removed the short cigarette drooping from his lower lip, extinguished it under one cracked boot, and went to answer the summons.

'Yes, Papa,' he said. His smart salute almost hit his forehead as he took in the grey-flecked beard which now concealed Kanekeh's chin and cheeks.

Through some mysterious prompting, Kanekeh had decided to keep the rank of sergeant that he attained in the national army, while conferring officer rankings on his young commanders. And since *they* knew hardly anything about the military apart from what their leader chose to tell them, it had not occurred to any of them to question the absurdity of taking orders from a mere sergeant. He made them drop their given names for assumed ones which he chose himself, naming Captains Rambo, Ninja and Dragon after greatly admired warrior heroes in the kind of video films that he once peddled. He chose Major Ironbone's alias to reflect that young man's exceptional physical strength, whereas Major Leopard's was meant to suggest his remarkable scouting and ambushing skills. Major Leopard and Captain Rambo, whose scouting skills were also considerable, led the PRA's reconnaissance details. Lieutenant Colonel (L-C) Pele, was a sniper who rarely missed his target. Kanekeh had named him after the legendary Brazilian footballer and Lieutenant Colonel (L-C) Fela, composer of the PRA anthem and other patriotic songs, after the renowned Nigerian musician of the seventies and eighties. And then there was Lieutenant Colonel (L-C) Odinga. *His* name belonged to an old Kenyan politician, Ojinga Odinga. Kanekeh had heard it on the radio some years before, and thought it sounded tough. The alias particularly suited this commander whom he had discovered living rough and independent on the streets.

The two most senior commanders were also the best educated, both having completed the first year of university before running out of money for tuition fees. Kanekeh named them after the most dreaded local snakes in the country. They were Colonels Cobra and Mamba. He had sent Colonel Mamba to set up a second secret camp called 'Justice' with Fela, Ninja, Dragon, Ironbone and roughly half of the remaining fighters, but maintained frequent contact with him by radio.

<><><><><><>

Like Cobra, the other commanders saluted smartly as they approached the porch where Kanekeh was sitting, quietly declaring, 'Power to the people!'

From his seat made of split bamboo strapped together with strips of a pliable bark, the PRA leader acknowledged the salutes with a careless gesture of his own and an equally indifferent response to the PRA slogan.

'Yes, yes, power to the people. '

Before the defeat that sent them fleeing to the forest, PRA fighters used to roar those words, but now, even if they had wanted to, they dared not say them too loudly for fear that the sound might betray their whereabouts to any enemy forces lurking nearby.

'At ease,' Kanekeh ordered. 'You may sit.'

He motioned them towards the uneven bamboo benches on the porch and straightaway, leaned forward, hands resting on solid thighs. They exposed badly scarred knuckles acquired when he was a boxer in the army. True product of mission schools and an environment where religious tolerance prevailed, as was his habit on these occasions, he began by intoning, 'Almighty God/Allah.'

The routine was so well known to the commanders by now that as if on cue, they dutifully bowed their heads.

'We always come to you with confidence because you are the Almighty king of justice and we know our cause is just. So many times in the past three years you have shown that you are on our side - those times when you put fear in the hearts of the government soldiers so that they ran away and left behind all their weapons and ammunition. Those times when villagers offered us food even before we asked them. Almighty God/Allah, you know what has happened recently. The tide has turned against us. But we have not lost heart. Not at all. We know this is only a temporary setback because you are just and our cause is just. Amen.'

'Amen,' muttered the men who considered themselves Christians, 'Amin' mumbled those who considered themselves Muslims, then raising their heads, they looked expectantly into the familiar yellowish eyeballs, brooding under heavy lids. Although three weeks of enforced inactivity and Kanekeh's total silence had been almost more than they could bear, none of them had thought to question him about the future of the movement. They knew that he would speak when he had something to tell them. Obviously, that time had come.

Kanekeh's eyes swept over the assembled commanders like a lighthouse beam, before coming to the point.

'Do you remember what happened the last time we engaged the enemy...?' he asked.

As if they could ever forget! Battle-hardened warriors though they were, some of them still shuddered at the memory of that terrible day outside Dembu when those helicopter gunships had appeared in the sky and swooped down to attack them with such deadly effect. Only sheer luck had saved them from being reduced to shreds of bone and flesh like their less fortunate comrades. Recalling the experience, they fidgeted on their seats.

'One thing is very clear,' Kanekeh went on. 'That is, that we cannot stand against helicopter gunships. At the same time, for the sake of the people of this country and for our own sakes, we *cannot* give up this struggle. So…the answer is to change our tactics and somehow force the new criminals in power to send the mercenaries away. But first I will have to get hold of more arms - as usual, friends of our movement will help with that when I contact them. The next thing we have to do is to start building up the PRA again. We have lost too many fighters...'

All the commanders were so absorbed by the speech that Cobra jumped when Kanekeh suddenly singled him out.

'Colonel Cobra... I am leaving you in charge. Your main assignment will be to find new recruits. When I return, which I hope will be in about six week's time, I expect to find many new PRA fighters even if you have to get them by force. And I want them to be ready to fight. Understand?'

'Yes, Papa,' Cobra replied, eager to please.

'You will have to think of a way to make them obey orders without question and to be loyal to the movement. Understand?'

'Yes, Papa.'

Turning his attention to the assembled commanders once more, Kanekeh inquired, 'Any questions?'

Several of the commanders would have liked to ask a question or two - such as how their leader was going to replenish their weapons now that they no longer had access to diamonds, and how he expected to bring arms into the country undetected when helicopter gunships were patrolling the sky. They also wondered why he had changed his mind about kidnapping recruits when he so often said in the past that conscripts were security risks in guerrilla warfare. However, having learned from experience that asking for questions was a mere ritual with their leader, they kept their queries to themselves.

'No questions?' Kanekeh asked again, and when no one answered, went on, 'Then that is all for today. I do not have to remind you that I expect complete cooperation with Colonel Cobra. L-C Pele, please set up the radio, I want to give Colonel Mamba the same instructions. You are dismissed.'

The commanders rose to their feet as one, muttered 'Power to the people,' saluted, and filed out into the pale streaks of sunshine filtering through the canopy above.

Kanekeh left the camp that very night, by what means or exactly when, none of his fighters knew, not even the lookouts. They guessed that he had left the camp only when they noticed his woman lying asleep on one of the benches outside his hut at a time of day when she would normally have been making a fire to cook him a meal.

This clandestine departure was nothing unusual, however. Kanekeh's habitual secretiveness and air of supreme confidence led his youthful fighters almost to believe that, like Moses the Israelite, their leader received direct orders from The Almighty and was answerable only to Him. As a result, they revered Kanekeh to the extent that even the recent reverses in battle and the ensuing difficulties of obtaining food and other essential supplies had not been enough to shake their conviction that they would win this war eventually. In any case, during his secret recruiting missions into the towns and villages where they once lived, Kanekeh had convinced them that their future well-being depended solely on the PRA waging a successful war against the government.

'It is the only way things can ever change for the better in this country,' he had told them, eyes blazing with the fire of conviction. 'The people in power now are criminals who care nothing about ordinary people like you and me. What they care about is making themselves rich and staying in power. That is all. Unless we, the ordinary people, take action they will remain in power until they die because the elections we have are just selections among their supporters.'

Kanekeh had won their hearts and minds by promising that once the war was over and won, it would be like brilliant morning sunshine appearing after a dark and stormy night. They would all be able to complete their education - free of charge, of course - and afterwards they would find employment - jobs that paid well, instead of passing their days the way he knew many of them did, wondering what life was all about; and in some cases, even wondering why they had ever been born.

Joining the PRA had given the young recruits a sense of purpose and pride, while providing them with excitement and adventure far beyond their most fantastic day-dreams. Some of those who lived in large towns before joining the movement had watched video films portraying the daring exploits of warrior heroes with names like 'Rambo' and 'The Dragon'. Now *they* were the fearless warriors themselves. It was an experience they found as intoxicating as the effects of the marijuana they cultivated and smoked regularly.

<><><><><><>

Once it was established that their leader had indeed departed, Cobra sent Leopard and his scouts to spy out the region around their camp and identify the villages most likely to yield a good harvest of conscripts.

'There are nine of them around here,' Leopard informed his colleagues when he returned four days later. 'But they will all have to be attacked on the same day, because they are very close together - not more than a mile or two apart. Otherwise the news will spread and most of the people will run away before we have a chance to get new fighters.'

'And what about government soldiers?' Colonel Cobra asked.

'We did not see any,' Leopard told him. 'Perhaps because we have been so quiet, they think the PRA is finished.'

That remark drew a deep and sinister chuckle from L-C Odinga. He could hardly wait to prove the government soldiers wrong. As a small lizard passed near his foot, he squashed it with one brutal stamp then casually tossed the bloody carcass into his mouth like a piece of chewing gum. None of his companions showed the slightest disgust at his action since they had all at one time or other eaten the raw flesh of all sorts of creatures. It was part of their training in jungle warfare and losing all sense of squeamishness had proved useful in the recent lean times.

'All right, thank you. Well done, Major,' said Colonel Cobra.

He thoughtfully drew on what was his last but one cigarette, blowing a cloud of foul-smelling tobacco into the air. 'We don't have much time before Papa returns, so we have to move fast. In fact tomorrow night we shall attack all the villages and towns Major Leopard has seen. Each of us will take forty to fifty fighters and carry only cutlasses and knives - no guns.'

Jerking his head in the scout's direction, he added with a lopsided smile, 'We have to be as quiet as leopards... and just as fast. Leave the older people and little children, but take all the young ones - girls as well as boys. Remember that our mission is to get more fighters and helpers for the PRA. I don't have to remind you to take any other useful things that we find, especially rice, kerosene and tobacco.'

'Don't you think it would be better to talk to the young ones and persuade them to join the PRA, instead of forcing them?' asked Fela the musician, who was at heart a peaceable individual. 'Like what Papa used to do before.'

'We don't have time for that now,' Cobra replied. 'You heard what Papa said. We have to use force.'

At the pleasurable prospect of bullying the weak into doing his will, Odinga chuckled again, his large, bulging eyes glittering like a glutton contemplating a feast.

Early the next morning they rounded up the remnants of the fighting force. Most of them, having spent part of the morning sweeping the clearing on which their camp had been set up, and cleaning those weapons that still worked, were now engaged in listless conversation and other idle pursuits. Thoroughly bored because they no longer had battles to look forward to, they rose sluggishly to obey their commanders' summons and had to be sharply reminded that they were still soldiers.

The PRA, once more than a thousand strong, now consisted of no more than five hundred fighters, divided between the two camps. None of the fighters was older than twenty-five and at least two dozen, were women and girls. Now that food and water were scarce, they had become a ragged, scrawny, smelly bunch. Except for the lucky few who owned battered sports shoes or boots, their dirt-encrusted feet were bare, or only partially protected by crude sandals made from old tyres, or by plastic flip-flops also caked with dirt. And except for those among them whose hair never grew more than a quarter of an inch, year in year out, they had to have their heads shaved regularly in order to keep lice and scabies at bay. Most of them covered their naked scalps with jaunty bandannas to make themselves look as stylishly reckless as some of their film heroes.

Just a few weeks earlier, these lack-lustre warriors had carried themselves with pride, AK-47 rifles dangling carelessly from their shoulders, bullet sashes bristling with cartridges slung across their chests over the juju charms many of them wore for added protection, their faith in their leader's invisible god being shaky at best. Now with many of their remaining weapons rusting in the makeshift shelters, they were a defeated army and looked it as they assembled in the open space in front of Kanekeh's quarters. In those thrilling days before the mercenaries arrived with their helicopter gunships, a meeting like this would have started with them singing the PRA anthem with all the energy they could muster. Due to concerns about security, the singing was now muted:

'The PRA is fighting to save our motherland.
The PRA is fighting to save our motherland.
The people will have food again,
The country will be saved.
The people will have work again,
The country will be saved.
The people will have health again,
The country will be saved.
POWER TO THE PEOPLE!'

The obligatory prayer followed, after which Colonel Cobra addressed the troops in his charge.

'All of you listen well,' he began. 'Papa has gone to find more arms for us. Before he left, he gave orders that when he returns he wants to see new fighters for the PRA. We only have about one month to get them and to train them, so we have to move fast...Hunting detail...'

A number of boys in their early teens separated themselves from the ranks, came forward and saluted, chorusing,

'Yessah.'

'Have you checked the traps yet?' Cobra demanded.

'Nosah,' they chorused again.

'Then do so at once.'

Always eager to observe what military etiquette they had learned, the boys said, 'Permission to leave, sah.'

'Yes, yes, go,' said Cobra, irritated by what he considered unnecessary formality.

'Cooking detail,' he called out as the boys trotted towards the tangle of vegetation beyond the clearing. A number of young women and girls in ragged blue jeans or combat trousers stepped forward. Their once white, but now greyish T-shirts hung shapelessly over their unsupported breasts. Two of them were clearly in the middle months of pregnancy.

'What is there to eat?' Cobra asked.

'Cassava, and green bananas, sah,' they replied.

'Enough for everybody?'

The girls in the cooking detail exchanged uncertain glances before the eldest of the group assured Cobra that they would manage.

'Good. Start getting ready to roast the cassava and bananas. If we are lucky, the hunting detail will find some sort of beef to go with it. You may go.'

Cobra now raised his voice to address the other young fighters who were eagerly awaiting more information.

'The rest of you are to collect all the cutlasses and hunting knives you can find, and sharpen them till they can cut thread. And we need rope - plenty of rope. Look for soft, tough plants like palms and vines and make as much rope as you can.' To their delight, he announced, 'We are going on raids tonight. Dismissed!'

Raids!! The prospect of action at last straightened the sagging spines of the fighters faster than any command could have achieved it. Apart from the excitement, raids meant fresh supplies - food other than cassava, as well as soap and kerosene and matches and salt - all the items they so desperately needed. A low buzz rose from the ranks before the troops dispersed. Eyes which had been dull just a little while ago now sparkled with anticipation, and previously dawdling feet moved swiftly to carry out the tasks that had been assigned. The cooking detachment lit fires in hollow ovens dug in the ground before going in search of broad coco yam leaves with which to wrap the cassava for roasting. They were hoping to find coco yams as well to add to the cassava. As ordered, the other young fighters took turns weaving ropes from tall grass, leaf fibres and vines and on sharpening the weapons they collected. They hummed intermittently as they worked so that harmonious sounds softened the rasp of metal against stone which went on for most of the day.

Night descended early and rapidly in the forest, and when it fell, no light penetrated the darkness even though the moon was almost full. Gradually birdsong and birdcall ceased as did the manic howls of monkeys crashing through the foliage far above them. Soon the only forest noises to be heard were eerie owl-hoots, bat-squeals, the distant cough of what might have been a leopard on the prowl, strange flutterings and twitterings overhead and rustlings in the undergrowth.

Refreshed by a few hours of sleep after a tasteless meal of cassava and wild coco yam accompanied by slivers of bush-hog and dwarf antelope harvested from the traps, the PRA fighters prepared for their expedition, then assembled in front of a small bonfire to invoke divine assistance yet again before breaking ranks to join the commanders to whom they had been assigned.

Accompanied by one of Leopard's scouts, L-C Odinga was the first commander to emerge from the forest with his raiding party; but the others were not far behind.

Chapter Five

DARK CLOUDS

20 November 1995

Went to see Belinda this p.m. Still not much progress with conversation; but enjoyed the visit all the same. Her younger sisters make me laugh, especially the one called Mimi. Her mother was just as cold as the last time when I greeted her; but at least she tolerates me in her house which is more than Melrose's father does for Khalid. He doesn't like the idea of his daughter having a Muslim boyfriend. He doesn't realise that he's only forcing Melrose to tell lies about where she's going and with whom.

When I was leaving, Belinda and I kissed on the stairs going down - a proper kiss involving tongues. She whispered, 'I love you.' I whispered, 'I love you too', but to tell the truth, I don't know what I meant, or what *she* meant, for that matter. I know that I like her, and that she is exciting, but do I *love* her? What is love anyway?

I think I am ready to meet my sister now.

29 November 1995

Went with Dad to see Melvina this p.m. Hesitated before telling Mams that I was going with him, but she said, 'Why not? She is your sister, after all.'

Impossible to deny who Melvina's father is - she looks just like Dad, and me - the same squarish jaw, but with cute dimples. If she lived with us, she would remind Mams every day of Dad's BIG SIN. Yet I'm sure Mams could love Melvina if she allowed herself to. Her grandmother left us together and Dad made her sit on his lap, but she only perched - as if she didn't want to be there. I felt very uncomfortable when she answered, 'Yes, Daddy, no, Daddy' to all his questions. As for me, I couldn't think of anything to say to her. Perhaps when she gets older....

On the way home Dad asked whether I thought Mams was coming round. Had to say I didn't think so, even though she has started making peppered fish for 'Millie's Corner' again. Dad gave a sigh that sounded as if all the air left his lungs. Hmm. One mistake long ago and three people miserable. I wonder if our family will ever be the same?

3 December 1995

Belinda's sixteenth birthday party. A day that will remain in my memory for as long as I live. I enjoyed the first couple of hours even though Belinda would not give me a straight answer when I asked her when she was going to cut her birthday cake. Around 10 o'clock, this guy comes in - at least 30 years old, smelling like a perfume shop, face powdered like a corpse, gold signet ring, medallion resting on his hairy chest. When he appeared, Mrs. Adams's smile stretched across her face from ear to ear, and she ran up to him, clapping her hands with delight and exclaiming, 'Ah, the very person we have been waiting for!'

She then invited him to cut the cake with Belinda. To be fair, Belinda looked very embarrassed, but she still held the knife with the guy and cut the cake. Afterwards he took her in his arms and kissed her on the lips for a long time. Everybody cheered and clapped, especially Mrs. Adams.

As soon as the dancing started again, I slunk away from the party feeling like a dog in disgrace, my tail between my legs. So upset that I could hardly breathe. I didn't even know Khalid had followed me till he called out my name. He walked part of the way home with me before going back to the party and his Melrose. He tried to make me feel better by saying '*Copain*, she's not worth it.' But he didn't succeed even though what he said is probably true. So humiliated, s*ooo* humiliated. Right now, I wouldn't mind being six feet underground.

5 December 1995

Belinda sent Chico to apologise to me on her behalf, making the excuse that it was all her mother's doing. I can believe that, but Mrs. Adams gave me a very clear message and I, Emmanuel Martin, will *never*, *ever* set foot in that house again. As usual Mams read me like a book, so I told her my sad story. She gave a funny, twisted smile and said, 'You are learning early that life is not a fairy story. Everybody finds that out sooner or later.' But then she rubbed my head the way she does when she's in a loving mood, and added, 'Never mind, sweetheart. There are plenty of other good fish in the sea.'

Hmm. Fishing is the last thing on my mind, right now.

25 December 1995

Going to bed early. This has been the worst Christmas day since the year Florrie died. Mams cooked the usual Christmas fare, but after dishing up, left the food on the table, covered with a country cloth and went to her room. At 4 p.m., I knocked on their door and asked about lunch. She just said, 'Serve yourself, Manny.' In the end Dad and I ate together but we had no appetite. Tried to make conversation, but he was not in the mood to talk either. Felt so downhearted that I didn't even feel like going up to the Noahs. Spent the rest of the afternoon sitting on the back steps with my Walkman, but even my new Koffi Olomide tape didn't sound as sweet as usual.

Thank goodness 1995 is almost over!! Apart from my 'O' level results, the only other good thing that happened to me this year is that no pimples have shown themselves for the past six months. Please God, let there be no more. Nasty, embarrassing things!

Chapter Six

KANEKEH'S SECOND REVELATION

Tropical rain forests evolved thousands, if not millions, of years before human beings ever thought of staking territorial claims; hence they have no respect for national borders. This explains how Kelli Kanekeh managed to slip into the neighbouring country where Malick had taken up residence, without meeting any border police or military patrols. In any case, he would probably have escaped detection, for none of the available photographs or wanted posters showed him with a beard of any description let alone the luxuriant growth that now covered half his face.

The journey took almost two weeks because he spent several days negotiating with known PRA sympathisers in villages along the way. These 'friends of the movement,' as he called them, while unwilling to take up arms themselves, were quite prepared to transport guns and other supplies to pre-arranged pick up points for small fees. Though Kanekeh realised that the likelihood of coming face to face with security patrols was small, he had also been extremely cautious in his movements, diving into undergrowth at the slightest unexplained sound and staying there till he was certain the danger was over.

Such anxious moments were at an end for the time being. Freshly showered and dressed in a new pair of jeans and a polo shirt in an attractive maroon colour, he was now sitting on a veranda on a hillside overlooking the Atlantic Ocean. With its highly polished black marble tiles, the veranda adorned a mansion built in a part of town known to the less well-to-do locals as 'the Cocaine Estate' because, so it was rumoured though unproven, all the owners of these opulent villas were or, like Malick, had once been, drug traffickers.

A tall glass of ice-cold Heineken beer stood untouched on the marble-topped table in front of Kanekeh who was deep in conversation with Malick. It was a heavier, more slack-muscled Malick these days for, unlike his friend and partner in insurgency, Malick had given up regular exercise, thinking that a man of great substance should look, well, substantial. To complete the image he wished to portray, whenever he was in Africa, he had taken to wearing loose white gowns very like those favoured by citizens of Saudi Arabia and states around the Persian Gulf .

'As we are speaking, my commanders are recruiting new fighters, but if I cannot provide more weapons and ammunition, we are finished,' Kanekeh told him.

Malick did not immediately respond to this remark because he was wondering glumly whether he and his partners would see any further return on their investment. The war had dragged on for three years and now the diamond fields had been retaken by the mercenaries hired by the government. With the advent of those deadly helicopter gunships, the likelihood of ultimate success appeared to be receding fast. Perhaps he and his associates would be wise to cut their losses before it was too late. As he pondered this predicament his eyes, resting on Kanekeh without seeing him, looked opaque and lifeless.

'My brother, getting more arms for you is not a problem,' he said finally. 'As you know, I have my regular contacts for that. The thing is, they are getting tired of waiting to see big profits. If you don't take back the diamond fields soon, you and I will have to think of another way to pay for this war.'

'Malick, I don't expect anybody to continue paying for our weapons forever,' Kanekeh said hurriedly. 'Those helicopter gunships are the only things holding us back. Once we get rid of them we shall start making progress again. You'll see. And when we take back the diamond fields, we shall pay all our debts and more. Why don't you let me talk to them myself? I know I can assure them that their investment is still safe.'

Malick dismissed that idea with an emphatic shake of the head, saying,

'No, they will refuse. They prefer to remain behind the scenes. That's how they operate.'

'Then, I beg you to trust me,' said Kanekeh.

'It's not a matter of trust, my brother,' Malick answered, averting his eyes to conceal his discomfort. In fact, his confidence in Kanekeh had grown over the years, ever since the PRA leader began to look and sound like a war lord and to display a remarkable ability to manage his troops and win battles. The new beard had also added an air of distinction to his confident bearing.

'I do trust you,' he went on, 'but I'm very worried about those mercenaries. How are you going to get rid of them? You told me just now that they nearly wiped you out ...'

'That is only because they took us by surprise,' Kanekeh replied smoothly. 'Don't worry. I am planning something. Just get the arms for me.'

Again Malick looked away, his expression still dark and troubled. Realising that the future of the PRA hung in the balance, Kanekeh leaned forward and fixed his eyes on his sponsor till Malick was forced to meet them.

'Trust me,' he urged when he knew that he had regained Malick's attention, 'Trust me.'

'Okay, but if you don't start making good progress soon, next time you will have to go to someone else for help...'

'That won't be necessary,' Kanekeh assured him. 'We are going to succeed. You will see.'

The two men settled down to talk business after that and discussed the types and quantities of weapons and ammunition the PRA required for future operations.

'And I also want something to make my boys more…more aggressive,' Kanekeh said, scowling and flexing his biceps to show Malik what he meant. 'Weed and the rum my woman makes are not powerful enough. I want those boys to become fierce and fearless - like hungry wild beasts.'

'For that, you need amphetamine capsules,' said Malick, who was by now an expert on the relative properties and costs of all the drugs on the market.' They will make your boys so strong that they will be able to fight for many hours without getting tired, and they will feel so powerful, they will be capable of anything… I can give you five thousand straightaway. I buy them wholesale in Thailand.'

'Wonderful!' Kanekeh exclaimed. He had no idea where Thailand was or what amphetamines were; nor did he care. All he wanted was to have at his disposal whatever was necessary to help him achieve his goal.

Thoroughly satisfied with the way the meeting had ended after its unpromising start, he reached out to grab Malick's hands which lay loosely clasped on the table.

'God will bless you, my brother!' he gushed. 'God will surely bless you!'

'Okay, okay... drink up, so we can go and eat.' Malick replied, slightly embarrassed by this outpouring of gratitude. 'Enough war talk for today....Fanta-ah…'

As if she had been waiting outside the door of the sitting-room for just such a summons, Malick's recently acquired fourth wife entered the lounge at once. She was a tall, biscuit-coloured Foulah woman who moved with the grace of a pampered princess, hitching the folds of a pink lace *boubou* over her elegant shoulders as she progressed with a light, swift tread across the lounge to the veranda.

'We are ready to eat now,' Malick informed her, and without a word or look she glided out again.

An hour or two later, having eaten his fill of steamed couscous and a well-seasoned chicken stew Kanekeh was in bed, but he lay staring at the ceiling even though the wide mattress embraced the contours of his body and quiet, split-level air-conditioning made the room delightfully cool. Despite his assurance to Malick that he had a plan, he had no idea how he was going to get rid of the mercenaries and their helicopter gunships. He realised that Malick meant what he said, about this being the last time he would help him with supplies; and who could blame him? Yet, for all that effort and risk to come to nothing! No, it could not be. As if to stimulate his brain, he hit his forehead with the heel of his hand, muttering, 'Think, Kanekeh. Think.' But inspiration, like sleep, continued to elude him. He threw aside the green satin bedspread covering his feet, went to the window and stared outside for a while, then turned away and paced the floor just as he had done in his quarters in the bush. However, when half an hour later, he found himself no closer to finding a solution to the problem, he returned to bed, and after tossing and turning for a while longer, eventually fell into a restless sleep.

He was standing over the lavatory bowl urinating copiously at daybreak, when an idea came to him at last. At first he felt that it was unworthy of a God-fearing man and rejected it at once, actually shaking his head vigorously as if doing so would dispel the wicked thought. It slithered right back, however, curled up in his mind and refused to budge. Terrorise the people, it hissed. Terrorise them till they run screaming to their MRC Chairman like stampeding cows. You will see. When that happens often enough, those guys will ask for negotiations. Then you can insist that the mercenaries fly back where they came from with their gunships before you will even *consider* talking. My friend, you cannot expect to harvest rice without hoeing the ground. You cannot prepare for a feast without slaughtering animals. Even if some people have to suffer now, their children and grandchildren will thank you in future.

The tempting thought persisted as Kanekeh stepped into the gleaming white shower stall and turned on the water. I have to concentrate on the goal, he told himself. The goal is what matters. Driving those thieves out; liberating the people; making our country better. And later, as he was doing his one hundred push-ups on the carpet another, even more potent, argument stole into his mind like a second sly serpent: After all, what did God Himself not do to the Egyptians when they refused to let the Israelites go? That teaches us that when the goal is worthwhile any action that will achieve it is justified. But He didn't terrorise the Israelites, Kanekeh reminded himself - only their enemies. That is not the point, the tempting thought insisted. His method worked.

PART TWO

Chapter Seven

THE PRA BACK ON ITS FEET

The door burst open like a clap of thunder, rudely interrupting Samu's gentle dream in which he was sitting on the river bank near the village, engaged in his favourite pastime - waiting for a fish to tug at his line. Amid the general pandemonium that ensued, he sat bolt upright on his mat, his heart hammering against his ribcage like a trapped bird. He was still in that position, looking about him in dazed confusion, when a kick landed against his ribs and knocked him sideways. Agony. He gasped and cried out, clutching his side.

His younger sister, Mawa, and his mother were wailing like new widows, while his little brothers aged four and two, made their own terrified contribution to the uproar.

Wide-awake now, Samu realised what was happening - that the dreaded PRA, labelled rebels and bandits by the government, had invaded their home. Despite the throbbing ache in his side, he sat up again and tried to scramble to his feet; but before he could move, a noose landed on his shoulders, slipped downwards and pinned his elbows to his sides. Invisible arms now dragged his back with Mawa, whom another of the intruders had ensnared and restrained in similar fashion. Their mother began a piteous appeal to the raiders, 'I beg you, don't harm my children. Please, don't harm my children.'

In response a harsh voice yelled, 'Out! get outside!'

Samu's heartbeats were thrusting against his ribcage even more forcefully, by the time their father appeared at the doorway to the only other room in the house. He was still under the influence of the two litres of palm-wine he had drunk before going to bed and swayed on his feet as he tried to secure a cloth loosely wrapped around his waist.

'Whatishappening? Whatishappening?' he mumbled.

'You will soon find out,' taunted a voice out of the darkness. 'Move!'

A booted foot lashed out at him with such force that the blow loosened the half tied cloth which fell away, leaving him naked. Trying unsuccessfully to keep his balance, he stumbled across the room and collapsed at the entrance to the house. For several minutes, he lay silent and still and, thinking he must have sustained a fatal injury, their mother let out such a shriek that Samu jerked against the rope restraining him. More terrified than ever, Mawa suddenly lost control of her bowels and the warm stench of fresh faeces floated upwards, further fouling the air which was already polluted by the smells of unwashed, sweaty bodies, aggression and fear all mingled together.

Samu could feel his sister's body quivering as she whimpered in helpless shame. And when, by the moonlight now streaming through the open doorway, he saw that there were three rebels, all armed with cutlasses, his own guts churned, threatening to give way too. Not even the secret rites he had undergone to mark his passage into manhood had frightened him as much as the sight of those menacing weapons and the desperadoes brandishing them.

The rebel still yelling at his mother now began to force her towards the doorway by squeezing the back of her neck, at the same time ordering the little ones to 'SHUT UP!' His bullying tone only made them wail louder as they stumbled after their mother, clutching at her wrapper. Still ignoring her pleas for mercy, the rebel snarled again like a bad-tempered dog, 'Move! move!' and kicked aside their father who was now sitting up in a dazed fashion, blocking the doorway. Samu's heart threatened to burst out of his chest since he was now certain that he and his sister were going to be treated in an equally callous fashion.

His state of quaking apprehension lasted another twenty minutes for with the adults out of the way, the rebels began to ransack the tiny house, searching every corner for anything worth stealing. Samu expected to hear them express disappointment when they realised that, like everyone else in the village, his family possessed little more than the bare necessities of life. Instead, each new discovery raised an exclamation of delight as if, far from being bare essentials, those everyday items were like gold nuggets - half a bucket of new rice, two large bunches of ripening plantains, a basket of smoked cat-fish, palm oil in a five-litre yellow plastic container, a box of matches, a bottle of kerosene almost full, and a couple of small tin lamps. In addition, their father's room yielded a small radio with two spare batteries, another box of matches, tobacco, a cutlass, plastic sandals and a stool.

Satisfied that the house had nothing else to offer, the rebels began carrying their booty outside. Mawa seized the opportunity to whisper a question to her brother.

'Samu...Samu...what do you think they will do to us?'

Unfortunately, one of the rebels returned sooner than she expected and heard the question. He supplied an answer that made both children gasp.

'You are going to become PRA fighters,' he declared.

Mawa immediately began to sob, but if she thought her tears would arouse the rebel's pity, she soon realized her mistake when he crossed the room in three strides and thrust his cutlass to within an inch of her face.

'SHUDUP,' he yelled. 'Just shut your mouth, you dirty, smelling thing. Shut your mouth!'

With one rough hand, he loosened the rope securing her to the post, and shoved her towards the porch where he had noticed a dented kerosene drum containing water.

'Wash your dirty self!' he ordered.

Sobs continued to shake Mawa's narrow shoulders, as she hastened to obey. She fumbled with her wrapper, trying to clean herself without exposing her body to her leering tormentor. At length she murmured, 'I have finished.' Whereupon, the rebel tied her up again, this time to one of the posts supporting the overhanging roof outside. He then returned to the house for Samu.

Meanwhile, with harsh words and brandished cutlasses, the rest of the raiding party were harassing the adults and infants they had chased from their homes.

'Your children are going to become PRA fighters,' they jeered at the parents brave enough to inquire about the fate of their older offspring, then cackled with even greater malice when this answer drew gasps and cries of dismay.

Some of the villagers went on to protest that the children were much too young to be fighters; to which the rebels carelessly replied that learning to become warriors would make them grow up faster.

'Anyway, it is your duty to let them go,' they added. 'After all they are going to fight for the country - to drive away those thieves and rogues that call themselves the government. Now get back inside!'

As if they had sprouted roots, the villagers did not budge until Odinga, for this was his unit in action, threatened to burn down their houses. Only then, did they begin to turn away, lamenting their fate, cursing the PRA and throwing backward glances towards the round, open-sided building which, under normal circumstances, served the village both as meeting house and school. It was there that the rebels had tethered Samu, Mawa and the rest of the children like a herd of goats while they prepared their ill-gotten gains for the return journey to the camp.

Those gains now included a good number of squawking chickens seized from household coops and tied together by their feet in groups of three or four which made them resemble bunches of some strange fruit.

'God will deal with you,' the villagers called out in futile rage; but far from being frightened by the threat, their tormentors seemed to find their expectation of divine intervention amusing.

'If that is what you think,' they scoffed, 'you are making a big mistake. God is on our side. We are fighting for our rights.'

Thirty minutes later, the unit started making its triumphant , if somewhat weary, way back to the camp, the entire operation having taken scarcely more than a couple of hours. The rebels stuffed rags in the children's mouths, then tied theirs wrists together before linking them in single file with ropes hung loosely around their necks.

Deeply traumatised by the events of the night it did not occur to the captives to try to escape. And even if it had, they would have found escape impossible since their captors outnumbered them by more than two to one.

<><><><><><>

'Just leave everything over there,' Odinga ordered, indicating the area outside their leader's quarters when they arrived at the camp. They had trudged through the forest for the best part of two nights, only stopping when the rebels sensed danger. After overseeing the removal of the captives' gags and restraints, Odinga selected three members of his unit at random, and ordered them to guard the newcomers.

'You can take it in turns to sleep,' he told them. 'Everyone else is to lie down quietly till the sun comes up... except...this one.'

There was no mistaking the voice that immediately let out a shriek, and Samu thought his heart would stop. He had heard such disgusting rumours about what rebel soldiers did to women and girls that he immediately assumed that Odinga was intent on raping his sister, Mawa. He started forward, yelling wildly in the direction of the rebel commander's retreating back, 'Leave her alone. She is only a child. Leave her alone....'

But if Odinga heard him, he gave no sign of it. It was the guard on duty who growled, 'You. Keep quiet and lie down before I show you pepper.'

Realising that he was powerless to save his sister, Samu sank to the ground, his chest heaving with suppressed anger and grief as Mawa continued to struggle and scream. Her efforts to avoid being dragged away served only to make Odinga dig calloused fingers harder into the tender flesh on the inside of her arm. Her shrieks grew louder, reached a peak of intensity, then began to diminish and finally ceased abruptly, as if a hand had been clapped over her mouth. Certain now that the rebel leader had killed his sister with savage lust, Samu shivered. His nightmarish experiences since the invasion of their village had left him exhausted yet he could not close his burning eyes. He spent the rest of the night staring into the darkness with his arms tightly wrapped around his knees.

<><><><><>

The idea of putting an identifying mark on the children came, not from the hard man Odinga, as might have been expected, but from Pele, the marksman. He suggested it during the early morning meeting to which Colonel Cobra summoned all the commanders. Its purpose was to review the previous operation and plan for the weeks ahead. Major Leopard thought putting a brand on another human being was contrary to the aims of the PRA as declared by their leader, and made his objections plain. He went on to point out that the children might fall ill as a result or even die if their wounds became infected, which would deprive the PRA of fresh fighters. Pele, however, remained firm in his opinion that it was the only way to prevent the conscripts from running away. To Leopard's frustration, everyone else seemed to agree with him; even Colonel Cobra who, while acknowledging that Leopard's fears were not unfounded, said, 'We shall just have to take that risk. We shall lose fighters as well, if they run away... and we shall also be putting ourselves in danger because they now know where we are. Suppose they bring government soldiers here?'

There was no need for him to spell out the consequences of any of the children leading government soldiers to their camp.

'Once they are labelled PRA, they will just have to stay with us,' he went on, and again all the assembled commanders except for Leopard, murmured and nodded their agreement. L-C Odinga even accused him of being too soft-hearted, to be a PRA fighter; but still deeply disturbed at the thought of torturing the innocent, Leopard continued to resist the idea.

'How can you be so sure marking will make them stay?' he argued. 'If it were me, I would try to run away no matter what you did.'

Cobra countered that argument by saying, 'We shall warn them that government soldiers are all over the place and that they kill anybody they think is a member of the PRA without asking questions. With the mark on their chest, they will not be able to prove that they are not PRA fighters.'

'And also, we can tell them that their families will not accept them any more,' Rambo added for good measure.

At that point, Leopard gave up trying to persuade the others to change their minds, reluctantly conceding that tough problems sometimes needed drastic solutions. But he asked to be excused from the proceedings. Much relieved that he had given in to the majority view Cobra, who preferred to lead by general consent, readily agreed.

'L-C Odinga, *you* begin,' he said. 'Let one of the fighters help you to hold the children down and cover their mouths so they cannot make any noise. When you are both tired, another two will take over, and so on till we finish.'

Reliving the particular delight of raping a virgin, and looking forward to more pleasures to come, L-C Odinga had been casually cleaning and trimming his dirt-encrusted fingernails throughout the meeting. Cobra was aware that he would never have dared to show such disrespect in Kanekeh's presence, but he concealed his displeasure, wishing to avoid conflict with a man whose violent nature he secretly feared.

L-C Odinga condescended to raise his head and asked,'Where do you want the mark to be?'

Squinting down at his own chest, Cobra spread tobacco-stained fingers wide over his breastbone. 'Right here...Make the cuts about three inches high, so the scars will be seen clearly.'

'It would be good if many of them have the same kind of flesh like mine that makes thick scars,' Odinga commented, tapping the shiny lump beside his left ear as he rose to his feet.

Samu was the first of the captives to be branded, simply because he happened to be sitting nearest to the bamboo bench which had been brought from Kanekeh's porch. Having ordered him to lie on the bench, the assistant made the mistake of concentrating on the victim's mouth, leaving his arms relatively free. He did not realise the wiry strength the boy had developed through helping his father slash tough grass and shrubs to prepare their farm for planting.

Samu knew that he could not possibly escape whatever fresh ordeal lay in store. Nevertheless, though terrified, he tried to put up a fight. He watched the commander approach the bench, holding a small knife with the blade pointing towards him, and glowing red-hot. Just as the blade began to descend, Samu shot out his right arm with the speed of a chameleon's tongue and grabbed Odinga's wrist. The commander jerked back, growling, 'Pay attention, you fool!' at his incompetent assistant. Samu tried desperately to hold on, but with two determined opponents, the contest was far too unequal to last more than a few seconds.

Afterwards, Odinga's big eyes looked down at the trapped boy without expression. Samu stared back, but his was the terrified gaze of a cornered animal.

'This one has to be taught a lesson,' Odinga said coolly and seared a diagonal line right across the boy's forehead.

Samu's whole body twitched like a dying chicken, so intense was the pain; but with his voice effectively silenced and his arms now firmly pinned to the bench, he could only moan deep in his throat as he writhed on the bench, blood dripping from his forehead like sweat.

The slight delay having cooled the metal, Odinga returned the knife to the flame once more before cutting the letters PRA into Samu's flesh. Mercifully, the boy lost consciousness before the commander started on the second letter.

The smell of charred flesh and the sound of moans and sobs were what finally roused him. Moaning and writhing himself, he looked from right to left in confusion, amazed to find that he was stretched out on the ground among many other boys similarly writhing and moaning and weeping. For a few bewildered moments he thought he must have undergone group circumcision with his age mates again. Then he remembered that this was an entirely different initiation, one conducted not by kindly, joking elders but by wicked rebels. More hateful recollections crowded his mind - the violent awakening in the middle of the night, the savage kick in his side, the abuse of his parents, the assault on his sister, the terrifying journey into the unknown with a rope around his neck... Would he ever see his home again? His family? His sister? Mental anguish sharpened the pain across his forehead and on his chest, making him cry out with the piteous yelps of an injured puppy.

He was still in that wretched condition when, following a courteous request for assistance from Colonel Cobra, Kanekeh's woman began moving round the wounded children with a plastic bowl containing freshly harvested honey. She seemed hardly more than a girl herself, tall and slender in a faded wrapper tied just beneath her armpits to preserve her modesty.

Crouching beside each suffering child, she whispered, 'Hush

now, hush,' as she dripped honey on their wounds to lessen the risk of infection. With a touch as gentle as her voice, her fingers moved lightly over Samu's skin, spreading the sticky fluid on the congealing blood. Her tenderness made him remember his mother's hands on his forehead whenever he had a fever and his entire body shook with silent weeping as the kind woman continued to pacify him. 'Hush now. It will soon stop hurting and you will be well again. You will see. Be a man.'

Her ministrations over, Kanekeh's woman returned to her quarters to continue awaiting his return. Other women and girls now appeared, these ones dressed in T-shirts and blue jeans or camouflage trousers. They brought water and a peppery soup in which floated bits of unidentifiable meat and small pieces of cassava. Samu managed to sit up and consume all that was offered in a few large gulps, but he felt extremely weak and immediately afterwards began to slump to the ground. That was when he caught sight of Mawa's cotton wrapper. She was lying some distance away, among a group of girls and though the movement of her limbs seemed as feeble as he felt, she was certainly alive. Samu's mind registered amazement that Mawa had survived all the sufferings she had endured since the rebels invaded their village, but he felt neither glad nor grateful. Nor did the fierce emotion of the previous night return. Enveloped in a cloud of depression by this time, he thought, 'What is the use of being angry?' They were truly prisoners now, himself, Mawa and the rest - slaves to be used and abused as their captors saw fit.

<><><><><>

Colonel Cobra passed the next few days in a state of intense anxiety that from time to time made him break out in a sweat and started a strange burning sensation in his stomach. His sense of responsibility weighed so heavily that he gave up all efforts to conserve the tobacco looted during the raid, and was constantly rolling cigarettes and lighting the new one from the stub of the last. And though he had ordered the camp girls and women to remain on the alert for signs of infection around the children's wounds, and for any sign of ants seeking the honey, he did several rounds himself to examine them. As Leopard had feared, a number of the young conscripts developed toxic fevers despite the honey salves, but having survived many bouts of diarrhoea and malaria since their infancy, these were hardy youngsters. With the help of bitter potions made from boiled roots which Kanekeh's woman concocted and the other young women gave them to drink at regular intervals, they gradually recovered.

By the fourth day Samu's skin was staying cool until evening when, for a few days more, a mild fever returned. His wounds no longer pricked and throbbed so badly. He now spent minutes on end, rubbing his chest and forehead with his fingertips in the way Kanekeh's woman had shown them to relieve the itching without damaging their skin before it was fully healed. As his health improved and he felt strong enough to sit up for longer periods, the resilience of youth reasserted itself. His depression began to lift despite the fact that the rebel commander's possession of Mawa appeared to be a permanent state of affairs and he was as ignorant as ever about what the future held in store for them.

He had had a few opportunities to talk to Mawa as he began moving around the camp, but on each occasion, she seemed reluctant to speak to him, her eyes darting here and there as if to make sure her master was not around. She had many duties, it seemed - fetching water from the stream, washing the rebel commander's clothes, bringing him his food and, what Samu hated to think about, sharing his sleeping quarters. Only God knew under what threats and abuse his sister was existing. The thought of attempting to escape crossed his mind more than once, but noticing how well the camp was guarded, he decided against it for the time being. In any case Mawa seemed so frightened that he doubted that she would be prepared to risk making Odinga angry; and he would never attempt an escape without her.

A week after their capture, Cobra Colonel ordered their heads to be shaved and their fingernails trimmed. Afterwards he gathered them around him and, to Samu's utter astonishment, began to pray for forgiveness. Samu's confusion deepened when the prayer ended; for Cobra now proceeded to offer his captives an apology.

'My name is Colonel Cobra,' he announced, looking the picture of kindly repentance. 'I want to tell you all that I am truly sorry for what we have done to you. I know you are thinking that we are wicked people; but we are not. We are only trying to bring change to this country. Change that will be good for everybody. All of us here joined the PRA of our own free will. Nobody forced us. The reason we had to capture you like that is because we need many more fighters to continue the war and there is no time now to go from place to place persuading people to join us. The government soldiers are pressing us hard.'

Listening attentively to this courteous speech, Samu found his hostility towards his captors waning a little, even though he did not quite believe Cobra's claim that the PRA were not altogether heartless. Not this commander perhaps, and possibly not most of the others, but as for that one - the one they called L-C Odinga - no one could tell him that he was not wicked. *He* was a devil.

Remembering the physical suffering he had endured, his hostility towards them all came flooding back as Cobra went on, in the same kindly tone, to explain why they had to be branded. They might not be altogether wicked, Samu thought, but they were certainly capable of extremely wicked deeds. And when the colonel then sternly threatened that if anyone tried to run away and was caught by the guards, his tongue would be cut out, Samu gasped in outrage. But then, having described the dire consequences the conscripts could expect if they did succeed in escaping from the camp and ran into government troops, Cobra again adopted a gentle tone as if to coax the kind of behaviour he desired from them. Samu felt certain that the colonel was deliberately playing with their emotions and came to the disgusted conclusion that whereas the commander, who had attacked his village was a devil through and through, this Colonel Cobra was a snake -- cunning and slippery.

'So I am begging you not to try to run away,' he was saying now. 'We do not want to you to suffer more than you have suffered already. All of us have to make a big sacrifice for the good of this country... In the coming days, the other commanders are going to teach you how to be fighters - everything you need to know to become first-class PRA members and fearless warriors. And you are going to enjoy the training, believe me.'

He made them rearrange themselves so that they stood in four rows of more or less equal length, then began assigning the rows to the commanders standing beside him.

'Captain Rambo, you will take the first row,' he said. 'This one...'

'*Please* let him not put me with that devil,' Samu prayed silently and fervently, his belly starting to churn at the thought of being put under the command of L-C Odinga. '*Please* let him not put me with that one. Please…'

'This one...L-C Pele. This one ... '

Samu thought the entire assembly must have heard his sigh of relief when Cobra put L-C Odinga in charge of the row before his own. *He* was going to be trained by a commander called, Major Leopard, a slight, muscular, brown-skinned man with narrow, twinkling eyes and one shoulder noticeably higher than the other.

Chapter Eight

GUERRILLAS IN THE MAKING

Samu was fortunate not only to have escaped having L-C Odinga as his instructor but to have been assigned to Major Leopard instead. In his previous existence Leopard had been a primary school teacher, one so comfortable in the class-room, that he had always believed that teaching was the reason for which he had entered the world. He answered Kanekeh's call to join the PRA only because his salary, paid by the government, had failed to materialise for eight months and he had too few private pupils to survive without it. He still missed his classroom after a four year absence and therefore welcomed any opportunity to practise his teaching skills.

'We are going to stay together night and day for the next four weeks,' he told his charges on the first day of their training, after leading them to a huge tree and telling them to make themselves comfortable under its branches. 'I want you to take me like your big brother, you hear? Listen well to everything I tell you, obey my instructions, and we shall get along fine. We are all one big family here... Now Lesson One. What is the PRA? And who is the leader of the PRA?... PRA stands for 'People's Redemption Army.' Repeat after me, 'People's …Redemption… Army.'

'People's Redemption Army,' said his pupils, stumbling over the words.

'Again...'

'People's Redemption Army.'

Only when Leopard was satisfied that the title was well implanted in the minds of the young recruits, did he move on to the second piece of vital information. 'And the name of our beloved leader is 'Kelli Kanekeh, Repeat…'

'Kelli Kanekeh,' chorused the new recruits.

'Again…'

'Kelli Kanekeh.'

'We call him 'Papa'. He has gone on a very important mission for us. That is why you have not seen him yet, but he shall soon return.'

And so the initial instruction progressed. Before the end of the day, Leopard had told them what the rebel movement was about. He had also taught them the PRA anthem by gathering them close around him and singing it softly over and over again. To teach them the rhythm of the song, he clapped quietly while moving his lopsided shoulders up and down in the manner of a familiar puppet. Even Samu chuckled at the sight in spite of his lingering resentment and fear.

Like the name of the insurgent army, the boys learned the PRA anthem by rote for even those among them who, like Samu, used to attend school, knew too little English for the words to make much sense. Leopard also made sure that they remembered the names and ranks of all the commanders and taught them essential military commands. He drilled them relentlessly, but with humour and ready praise, till they stood and marched like pint-sized soldiers.

Despite his suspicion that, being a PRA commander, Leopard was at least capable of wickedness, Samu felt drawn to his instructor. By the end of the third week of training this attraction had developed into full-blown hero-worship. In his present circumstances, he wanted nothing more than to please Major Leopard and for that reason was determined to do well.

That was the week Leopard began to teach them the basics of guerrilla warfare. Samu found this new knowledge so exciting that he enjoyed re-running the events of the day in his mind as he waited for sleep - Leopard entering the forest ahead of them and leaving many small signs of human activity, then teaching them to recognize the clues - disturbed undergrowth, the ground depressed by footprints, tree barks dripping sap, freshly broken twigs. He taught them to move as stealthily as cats and to attach trip-wires to grenades and hide them in the ground to ambush the enemy. They learned to imitate the soft call of doves and use it to keep in touch with each other when lying in wait for the enemy. Having no experience of the dangers of war, Samu began to look forward to the time when he would be able to put into practice all that he had learned.

Finally it was the last week of instruction. Leopard told them that they were now going to learn how to handle an AK-47 which was the gun PRA fighters used, though they would not be able to fire it for the time being. The enemy were too close and they would not have a new supply of ammunition till 'Papa' returned. He summoned three seasoned fighters to assist with this part of the training and having introduced them as 'Your brothers Lans, Samson and Zig,' again drew smiles and chuckles from his trainees by going on to inform them, with a great show of admiration, that what Lans, Samson and Zig did not know about AK-47s no one else in the world did - not even the people who made the guns.

AK47s were Kanekeh's weapons of choice for several excellent reasons. They were among the cheapest automatic assault weapons on the market, light enough for an army moving on its feet most of the time, simple to operate, clean and repair and above all, reliable. Furthermore, it was possible to purchase a thousand rounds of ammunition for as little as one hundred US dollars.

Kanekeh's army could also boast of a quantity of hand-held, rocket-propelled grenade launchers or RPGs as they were commonly called. These were lethal against troops like the national army, which lacked protective vests and used the old type of armoured vehicles which were relatively easy to penetrate. RPGs were also reasonably inexpensive, yet too costly to be distributed to more than a few crack shots like L-C Pele. New recruits did not have to learn how to handle them.

Samu's instructor was the fighter Leopard had introduced as 'Lans' - a short, muscular, youth with a hard, unfriendly face. He disassembled his AK47 with a speed that appeared magical to the new recruits, then re-assembled and disassembled it again before spreading the pieces on the ground and naming them one by one, '... magazine, bolt, bolt-carrier, bolt-carrier lever, chamber, gas tube...' Afterwards he lowered his bandanna to cover his eyes and went through the entire process again.

'That is what you people have to be able to do,' he told his awed audience, 'and you have to do it in one minute.'

Open-mouthed, the boys looked at each other with wide-eyed

dismay which made Lans chuckle condescendingly, repeating, 'Yes, one minute.'

It seemed impossible at first, but in a few days they were consistently identifying and naming all the parts of an AK-47. The disassembly/re-assembly routine took longer to master even though they were all used to manipulating fishing-lines and hooks and fiddling with pieces of wire to set traps in the bush. Samu had less difficulty in accomplishing the blind re-assembly routine because he had one big advantage over his fellow-recruits - a photographic memory which permanently fixed objects in his mind once he had examined them closely. Last thing at night he visualized the gun and its components, and lined them up mentally to name them one by one. All the same, he only managed to carry out the disassembly/re-assembly routine in three minutes the first time he tried though, to his delighted surprise, Lans eyed him with new respect and not a little suspicion.

'*You* learn fast-oh!' Lans remarked. 'It took me more than five minutes the first time.'

He did not report this astonishing progress to Major Leopard, but the instructor soon discovered Samu's ability when he tested the recruits himself.

'God must have made you to be a soldier,' he exclaimed, his eyes sparkling. 'From now on I will take you with me when I go on special operations. All of you clap for him.'

No one noticed that Lans did not join in the applause.

As he basked in his hero's approval, Samu sharply regretted the absence of his parents, especially his father who had often accused him of being lazy because he spent so much time sitting on the edge of the river bank waiting for fish to take his bait. This reminder of the circumstances in which he was learning to be a warrior dampened his spirits, but did not entirely extinguish his pleasure.

<><><><><><>

Meanwhile, a completely different scene was unfolding at the far end of the camp. Since he was not involved in training the recruits all day,

Cobra had decided to keep the idle fighters busy by improving accommodation in the camp. They were building three new dormitory shacks of plaited palm fronds to house the new recruits and any more to come. To keep the youths attentive to their work, Cobra was in the habit of arriving unannounced at the various construction sites. It was during one such visit to one of the half-completed huts that he discovered three little boys who were supposed to be undergoing training. They jumped to their feet as he approached and tried to scurry to the back of the hut, but he caught one of them by his skinny arm and pulled him back. The others followed, dragging their feet.

'What are you doing here?' Cobra demanded. 'Who is your trainer?'

The recruits hung their heads in silence until one of the boys thatching the roof of the hut, volunteered the information that they were all with L-C Odinga.

'They were not doing well, sah, so he says they have to be porters.'

That is *not* his decision to make, Cobra thought irritably. Then he noticed tear-streaks on the boys' dirty faces.

'Is that why you have been crying like babies?' he demanded.

Again the answer had to come from the helpful builder.

'They are wounded, sah.'

'Wounded? Where?' Cobra snapped.

On closer inspection, he saw that the boys had been lashed across their legs hard enough to draw blood in several places. Cursing Odinga under his breath, he turned and strode purposefully away in search of the culprit. A confrontation with Odinga had now become inevitable for he realized that he could not withhold condemnation of such brutality and keep his self-respect.

On finding the commander idly inhaling marijuana in front of his shelter, Cobra growled, 'L-C a word please - on Papa's porch,' and walked away before the commander could react to the summons.

Several minutes passed before Odinga sauntered on to Kanekeh's porch, making Cobra feel even angrier. He immediately went on the attack.

'L-C Odinga, were you not listening when I spoke to the new recruits last month?' he demanded. 'Did you not hear me apologising to the boys for causing them pain?'

As Odinga's expression darkened, Cobra began to feel the burning sensation in his stomach again. However, he carried on with all the severity he could muster.

'We marked the boys, but that was so they would not run away. Now that they are being trained, I want them to be treated like human beings, not like dogs. After all, they are people's children.'

'Why are you making all this palaver?' Odinga retorted. 'I only gave them a few lashes to make them learn faster. Teachers do that all the time...'

'It is not a matter of the number of lashes you gave them, Odinga,' Cobra pointed out furiously. 'You *wounded* them - you drew their blood.'

'For a good reason. We are fighting a war. They have to be tough.'

'Yes, but we don't have to treat them like slaves,' Cobra told him. 'I have not said anything about the little girl because you did a good job that night, but I will not allow that kind of beating, you hear me?'

'And how are you going to stop me?' Odinga replied, coolly removing another marijuana cigarette from his breast pocket. He lit it and inhaled deeply, all the while looking his superior commander straight in the eye.

Such insolence from his junior in rank left Cobra speechless with rage for a moment, and when he felt able to speak again, he had difficulty steadying his voice.

'L-C Odinga,' he began, then paused to take a deep breath. 'have you forgotten that Papa put me in charge of this camp in his absence? Do you remember what he said? I shall have to report you for this.'

'And you will live to regret it...'

Cobra's heart was already pumping hard and the thought of making an enemy of this violent man now made his heartbeats skip and race. Nevertheless, he felt strangely light-hearted.

Just then, Kanekeh's woman emerged from within carrying a

bundle of clothes. Recognizing a familiar patterned shirt, for a moment the warring parties stared at each other dumbfounded before, stating the obvious, Cobra murmured,

'Papa has returned. He must have heard everything.'

Chapter Nine

THE RETURN OF KANEKEH

'Colonel Cobra!'

It was the next morning. Cobra had been expecting to hear that bellow at any moment once he realized that Kanekeh had returned and the thought of having to report L-C Odinga's offence had made him jumpy for the rest of the previous evening and kept him awake for half the night. As his indignation cooled, his reluctance to make an enemy of Odinga returned so that he almost succeeded in convincing himself that it would be better to lose self-respect than to live in anxious anticipation of Odinga's revenge. Indeed, had he not been so certain that Kanekeh overheard their bad-tempered exchange, he might have given in to a temptation to drop the matter.

He took a last quick drag on his cigarette before pinching it out and putting it into his breast pocket. It would taste foul the next time he lit it, but he had just taken a few puffs and cigarettes were too precious to waste.

Kanekeh was sitting on one of the bamboo benches outside his quarters, facing the light. The moment Cobra laid eyes on him again he realized that their leader had changed in some fundamental way though, even if pressed, he could not have said exactly what made him come to that conclusion. It was something to do with his eyes, perhaps. They now held a strange light - a deep glow which Cobra had never noticed before. He even wondered whether Kanekeh might have started taking drugs, but knowing the leader's habits, dismissed the idea as being too unlikely. There had to be another reason.

'You are welcome, Papa,' he said after the usual salute.

'Thank you,' Kanekeh smiled. 'Let me have your report. We shall pray later when the others have joined us... Start with the recruitment. How many new fighters do we have now?'

'One hundred and ten, Papa,' Cobra informed him. 'Sixty here and fifty at Camp Justice.'

'Hmm. Not as many as I hoped....'

'We did our best, sah.'

'No, no - I am not criticising you,' Kanekeh hurried to assure Cobra. 'I have no doubt that you did your best. In any case that number will do for now - combined with the ones we have already. How far have you gone with their training?'

'Very far, Papa, very far. In fact, basic training is now complete... But before that we had to take a decision... '

'Yes?' Kanekeh inquired.

'Well... because we had to take the recruits from their villages by force, we had to make sure they would not try to run away...'

'And...?'

'We decided to mark PRA on their chests, sah. We... we cut them,' Cobra stammered, wondering how Kanekeh would take the news.

To his bewilderment, for the former Kanekeh would never have learned of injury to his fighters without at least expressing regret, the leader's response to this information was remarkably indifferent.

'If you thought it was necessary to cut them, I go with your decision,' he said. 'Did any of them die as a result?'

'O, no, sah. They have all recovered. Madam helped us to look after them.'

On hearing this, a fond smile played around Kanekeh's lips, revealing traces of the more benign character Cobra was used to.

'Yes, she's very good at that,' he remarked. 'Anything else?'

'We have been expanding the accommodation in the camp, sah - four new quarters are almost completed.'

'*Very* good. What about discipline -- did you have any problems?'

'Only one, sah,' Cobra said after a moment's hesitation. 'I had to reprimand L-C Odinga for flogging three of the new recruits in a very brutal way.'

Reporting the episode fanned the dying embers of his anger, hardening his voice as he went on, 'He beat them till they bled...'.

Kanekeh's calm acceptance of the branding of the recruits, should have alerted Cobra to the possibility of an equally surprising response to his report of L-C Odinga's cruelty; but he was again puzzled and dismayed when the PRA leader merely pursed his lips thoughtfully after saying, 'Hmmm.'

Could this be the same Kelli Kanekeh, Cobra wondered in confusion. On more than one occasion, Kanekeh had told his commanders that if they had to discipline any of the fighters, they should try not to be too harsh. 'I want us to be one big family,' he had said, 'just as I want our country to become one big family.'

'All right, call the others now,' Kanekeh said. 'I want to brief you on the new tactics I have in mind.'

As he went to carry out the order, it dawned on Cobra that the change apparent in their leader was going to affect the PRA, and in a way which he might find difficult to accept. The customary prayer before the briefing did nothing to dispel this sense of foreboding for after invoking 'Almighty God/Allah' as usual, Kanekeh's prayer continued in this way:

'I come to you with a grateful heart because of your protection and guidance throughout my mission. Thank you for all the assistance you have given our movement. Almighty God/Allah, you have shown us by your example in the Holy Bible, that sometimes it is necessary to commit acts that people consider wicked in order to achieve something good. We will follow your divine example and do whatever is necessary to save this country from the evildoers that rule over it. We only pray for courage. Amen.... Right. Sit up straight and listen well.

In three weeks time, our new supplies will arrive. They are coming by canoe, and Colonel Mamba will organize transport to the two camps since Camp Justice is nearer the river. As far as the war is concerned, our next task is to recapture the diamond fields - that is priority number one. However, since we cannot stand against helicopter gunships, the only way we can succeed is by making sure there are none of them within the borders of this country. So - we shall have to do some evil that good may come. That is what I was referring to just now in my prayer. We have to become very nasty to the people around here. Very, very nasty; and we shall continue to be nasty till the MRC agree to negotiate with us. When they do, my first demand will be for the gunships to leave the country. They will accept this demand in the end. Once the gunships are not here anymore, there will be no problem taking back the diamond fields. Those army boys are no match for us...

Any questions so far? '

The way Kanekeh's eyes flashed and he distorted his lips when saying the word 'nasty' suggested that what he had in mind were acts of savage cruelty. With each repetition of the word, Cobra had become more alarmed and by the end of the briefing felt disturbed enough to summon up his uncertain reserves of moral courage without too much of a struggle. Raising a hand, he said, 'Papa, excuse me for asking, sah...'

All heads turned in his direction - his fellow commanders with raised eyebrows and, in the case of Leopard, open admiration at his daring. Kanekeh acknowledged the request with a slight frown of irritation and a little tremor rippled across Cobra's abdomen. However, he continued resolutely enough.

'Can we be sure that things will work out like that? Suppose the MRC decide to be tough, no matter how much we attack the villages. How long are we going to continue to be - as you said - nasty to innocent people?'

Kanekeh's response was a patronising chuckle.

'Heh, heh. Heh, heh. First of all, you would not be asking me that if you had any knowledge of the world outside this country. Have any of you heard of the United Nations?'

'Yessah,' Cobra replied, but in a tentative way since he had no idea where that question was leading.

'Well, at the United Nations they are always talking about what they call 'human rights'. When they find out how much innocent people are suffering here and that the reason we are attacking them is because the MRC government refuses to negotiate with us, they will force the MRC to negotiate with us. You will see. First they will condemn our behaviour and call us savages, then they will criticize the MRC using strong words and then pass a resolution to squeeze them more... They won't be allowed to travel, or to buy weapons, and so on and so forth...Meanwhile, *we* shall keep on saying we are ready to negotiate - once the mercenaries are gone. Mercenaries don't have a good name anywhere. As for how long we will continue being nasty to innocent people?... For as long as it is necessary. This has to be 'Operation no mercy.'

Like Cobra, Leopard listened to Kanekeh spelling out the new PRA strategy with rising alarm and a good deal of confusion. Alarm, because he wanted no part in deliberately injuring unarmed people, and confusion, because he could not understand how Kanekeh could be planning to inflict such suffering on the very people for whom they were supposed to be fighting. When he could contain his misgivings no longer, *he* also raised his hand and asked to speak.

'Papa, excuse me,' he said, hesitantly. 'I am confused. Will we not be going against the beliefs of the PRA if we behave like that?'

Kanekeh's frown deepened. He had already taken a breath to reply when L-C Odinga raised his hand.

'Major,' he said, 'have you forgotten what you yourself said when we were talking about marking those boys... that tough problems sometimes call for tough solutions? As I see it, we have no alternative.'

Pele and Rambo nodded in agreement but Cobra's face revealed nothing - a fact that did not escape Kanekeh's notice. As had happened on that earlier occasion, Leopard persisted in opposing the new tactics, arguing passionately that the PRA would also lose support if its fighters attacked the very people they were fighting for. Kanekeh cut him off in mid-sentence to say, 'You have made your point, Major Leopard.' At first appearing to joke, he added mildly, 'And you also sound as if *you* are the leader of the PRA.' Then all of a sudden, his countenance changed again and he glared from one to the other of the two commanders who had dared to question his decision.

'Let me remind you both, Cobra and Leopard, that *I* am the founder and leader of the PRA movement and commander in chief of this army. I make decisions as I see fit. By the time I call you people for briefing, I have thought long and deeply and I have considered every angle - the reasons for and the reasons against any action. Don't think I no longer believe in all the aims of the PRA. I do, but right now, the most important thing is winning this war. We have to put such ideals to one side for the time being. Meanwhile, I will not tolerate any more arguments over what tactics to use. You hear me?'

Heads bowed, the two commanders muttered their apologies, acutely aware of the threat in their leader's voice.

'You are both good men and I know that you are sincerely dedicated to our movement,' Kanekeh continued less harshly, 'but after the way you have spoken today, I don't think I can rely on you to put your hearts and minds into 'Operation no mercy'. For that, I need people with more fire in their bellies than the two of you. People who won't hesitate to do whatever is necessary to achieve our goal; so until further notice you will both be responsible only for managing the camp... Pele... radio Camp Justice for me. I want to talk to Colonel Mamba about the supplies. L-C Odinga, you will stay behind for further briefing. I am putting *you* in charge of 'Operation no mercy'. The rest of you are dismissed...O, and I want to meet our new fighters. Let them assemble outside and wait for me.'

<><><><><><>

Samu did not know what to make of the short, tough-looking man strutting towards them in his laced up canvas boots, combat uniform and a soft peaked cap of the same green and khaki camouflage material. He acted like a jovial relation as he moved through the ranks of new recruits, stopping to stroke a chin here, to rub a shiny scalp there and to crack little jokes. His tone was kind when he asked what had caused the pinkish scar streaking Samu's forehead, but he did not wait for an answer, which made the boy distrust him as much as he did the other commanders, Leopard excepted. This was their leader, after all - the man who started the war.

The inspection over, Kanekeh raised his voice in one of his fervent prayers to 'Almighty God/Allah', pleading for the protection of 'these brave young people fighting to save our country.' He then declared, 'From now on *I* am your father, do you hear? I will look after you just like a father. But you have to be very obedient - both as my children and as PRA soldiers. Completely obedient. If you do not do as you are told, and without any argument, you will be punished. And let me warn you - military punishment is tough. Very, very tough. We are fighting to make this country a better place for everyone, and you must be ready to play your part... Now let me hear you sing, the PRA anthem, but not too loudly,' he added, lowering his voice in a dramatic way. 'Our enemies are all around.'

'Wonderful!' he beamed when the garbled rendition came to an end and strode back to his quarters, slapping his stick against his sturdy thigh.

<><><><><>

Ever since hearing that they would soon be going on an operation, Samu's emotions had swung between anxiety and excitement. Anxiety, because he had no idea what the mission would entail, and excitement because he thought it would provide an opportunity to practice some of the skills he had lately acquired. When it emerged that they would be raiding a village and L-C Odinga would be in charge, the balance tipped towards anxiety and remained there - mouth-drying, stomach-churning anxiety. He recalled the way Odinga and his unit had behaved during the raid on his own village a few weeks before, and feared that he would soon be expected to act with similar cruelty or else face severe punishment which he had no doubt would be inflicted by that devil himself. He would have given a week's rations and more to be going on the raid with Major Leopard instead, because he felt certain that though his hero would carry out Kanekeh's orders, he would do so without enjoyment. However, Leopard was obviously taking no part in the planned raid. He had been sitting under the flamboyant tree playing draughts with Colonel Cobra for most of the day. Samu also observed that one game succeeded another with unusual restraint between the players. He had the impression that they were merely killing time.

As the forest shadows deepened, Odinga assembled his unit, pushing, shoving and barking orders at the boys.

'Line up, line up, then come to me one at a time.'

He began to hand out brown capsules from a crumpled packet - the amphetamines Kanekeh had acquired from Malick.

'They will make you as strong and as fearless as leopards,' he said with impish humour when some of the boys hesitated to take the capsules from him. 'Swallow them with rum from that bucket over there

- but only half a cup, mind.'

The 'rum' was a potent brew distilled by Kanekeh's woman from wild berries and he wanted them only slightly intoxicated,

The older boys did as they were told, slapping their chests and grunting like the experienced drinkers they were, and the newly trained fighters followed their example. However they soon discovered that those rituals did little to help ease the passage of the fiery liquid down their throats. Many of them coughed and gagged and had to wipe streaming eyes; but within ten minutes L-C Odinga was pleased to observe that the combination of the capsules and alcohol was having the desired effect. All the boys seemed to be standing taller and almost vibrating with energy. Armed only with knives and cutlasses as they had been on the previous raid, some of them started thrusting these weapons at each other, stopping just short of inflicting stab or slash wounds, while others twirled around slicing them through the air as if taking swipes at long grass.

'Enough,' L-C Odinga ordered after a while. 'Let us start moving out.'

He tossed a couple of the capsules into his own mouth and took a large swig of alcohol, relishing the prospect of the mayhem ahead. There would be no chicken-hearted hesitation among any of the boys in his unit when the time came for action. He was certain of that.

<><><><><><>

The moment his eyes fluttered open, Samu smelled blood. His left temple throbbed painfully while the inside of his mouth tasted as if something had died there. Suddenly his stomach heaved, giving him hardly any time to dash outside the shelter before a bitter liquid spewed up over the fingers of his right hand which he had clamped over his mouth. As Samu continued to retch, the guard on duty growled unsympathetically, 'Make sure you clean up your mess properly or else I will deal with you.'

Having done his best to obey the order, Samu dragged himself back to the hut and sank to the ground. He shut his eyes again but knew that he would do no more sleeping that night. In fact, he wondered whether he would ever sleep again without having nightmares. Only sheer exhaustion had knocked him out when they returned to the camp after the raid.

He lay in the darkness wide awake as shrieks of horror mingled with moans of pain, pleas for mercy, blood-chilling whoops and obscene language echoed and re-echoed in his head. Horrible images crowded his ravaged mind which pictured them more vividly than they had been at the time, even when the blazing houses - their final atrocity - had imparted a reddish glow to the scene. Bloody gaps where lips and ears and noses had been. Stumps dripping blood where hands and feet had been. Two pregnant women dying on the ground, the contents of their bellies spilling out, their wombs split open - pitiful little corpses curled up beside them, still attached to their umbilical cords. He could not remember exactly what part he had played in the carnage, but knew for certain that he had acquitted himself well enough not to fear having to face any punishment. He remembered that L-C Odinga, baring his gappy teeth in a satisfied grin and waving his bloody cutlass over his head, had congratulated them all, saying, 'Papa will be very pleased with this unit.'

It now struck Samu like the sting of a slap that his forced participation in the raid had settled his future once and for all. He was now a fully-fledged PRA fighter, as much a vicious outlaw in the eyes of the government and the people, as the commander he so detested. In despair, he felt like tearing his heart out, but did not weep. Instead, the scars on his chest and forehead began to itch and burn - only slightly at first - then they stung as if biting ants had invaded the shelter. The intense irritation rapidly grew worse, then so unbearable that he had to bite his lower lip to stop himself from crying out. Desperately seeking relief, he dug his nails into his tortured skin - head, chest, head, chest and scratched until he felt the wetness of blood on his fingers. When morning came, his bandanna pulled well down and his hands holding the lapels of his shirt together, he hurried down to the stream by the camp to wash himself before anyone noticed his strange injuries.

He was in the process of splashing water on his face when he came to the painful conclusion that his present predicament must have been his destiny from birth, just as Major Leopard had said. Unlike Major Leopard and most of the others, he had not chosen to join the PRA. He had been forced into it, tethered like a goat, then drugged and made to commit those terrible crimes. The more he dwelled on the situation the more anger he felt, not only at the injustice of fate but also against himself for not being able to escape it.

By the time he had finished washing himself, he was seething with anger, though no one could have guessed it for his face betrayed nothing of his inner turmoil. But this rage accompanied him wherever he went, like an aggressive dog kept on a chain until circumstances permitted it to be let loose - in this case, during the frequent raids demanded by 'Operation no mercy.' Before long, hating his victims for their weakness as much as he hated himself, Samu was slashing and burning, killing and maiming almost as recklessly as L-C Odinga, the commander he so despised.

Chapter Ten

BREAKS IN THE CLOUDS

5 January 1996

I wonder what is happening up-country. No war bulletin for some time now. Before that they were still only reporting 'mopping up operations'. Perhaps like that soldier said, the war is almost over. Am I glad or sorry? Mixed feelings. The IDPs upset me, but it was exciting to see the military lorries and helicopters going up and down. People are now saying that the MRC have started behaving exactly like the previous government. That their wives and girlfriends all have cars, that mansions are going up all over the place as if by magic, and that they bully people all the time - even humiliating big people in public. Electricity supply has deteriorated again, and as for the new water pipe they said was coming this way, forget it.

20 January 1996

Dad was in very low spirits this evening because of an incident he witnessed on his way home from work. Some soldiers driving down a one-way street at breakneck speed and in the wrong direction, lost control of their jeep, killed an old beggar and badly wounded a woman selling '*fry-fry*' by the roadside. What upset Dad more was that the soldiers didn't even bother to stop.

He described the incident to nobody in particular when he entered the house, as if he just had to get it off his chest. Mams promptly put her hands on her head, crying, 'Oh, our poor country!'

In spite of my own disgust at what had happened, I felt happy because Mams had reacted to something Dad said instead of ignoring him, as she has been doing for months. It was like a glimmer of light in cold darkness. Perhaps...Hmm. Let me not raise my hopes yet.

Gramma Cobola said her bones were aching badly again so I had to work in 'Millie's Corner.' A hot, hot argument began after beer and stout had been flowing for a while because of what people fleeing from up-country are saying. The latest is that the PRA are now attacking villages and burning them to the ground, killing unarmed people in their beds and abducting boys and girls. They say PRA fighters are raping women in front of their husbands and children - even old women, and are calling their brutality 'Operation no mercy.' I have been shocked to the core by all the reports, but had to smile when I told Dad that I no longer supported the war. Forgetting that he isn't a believer, he said, 'Thank God, you have come to your senses, Manny!'

He looked a bit embarrassed when I teased him about it, then told me it was an automatic response.

These PRA people sound worse than any government we have had so far. If they win this war it will be a matter of the devils we know being replaced by devils we would be better off not knowing. Despite the terrible reports, some of Dad's customers still insisted that they were in favour of the war. When others challenged them, they simply shrugged their shoulders and said, 'War is war - bad things happen in wars. Look what happened in Biafra… The PRA are fighting for a good cause.'

The group against the war said that attacking helpless people was wickedness and thuggery (my view exactly) - that fighting a war should be between armies, no matter what the issue. The argument went back and forth, back and forth like a table tennis ball, everyone shouting and sweating more and more. It took a different turn when the pro-rebel group said it was wrong of the MRC to bring white mercenaries to fight against their own brothers - Africans like themselves. The anti-rebel group said the MRC had promised to end the war and they were only trying to keep their promise. That was no excuse, said the PRA supporters. They should not have brought white people into a quarrel among Africans. Dad simply listened to them arguing until it almost ended in a fight; then he became so alarmed that he told them to drink up and go. That started another argument - this time with him for being 'so difficult.' Fortunately things calmed down in the end, otherwise, I don't know what would have happened since we don't have a police-station around here.

22 January 1996

Went with *les copains* to the Town Hall to listen to a talk by a very strange man - Mr Azigidah from Ghana. Dark as midnight and almost a giant in a hand-woven tunic -- black and white, with a cap to match. He carried a black walking stick with a brass handle shaped like a lion's head and had a big gold-looking medallion on a dark cord round his neck. It was shaped like a map of Africa. Except for his colour, Mr Azigidah reminded me of the picture of Jeremiah in my Bible - eyes blazing and very serious. A powerful speaker too. Says he has started a group to resurrect black Africa and he is going around the continent talking to young people because *we* are the future. He wrote the name of the group: NEW AFRIKANS on a flip-chart. According to him, that is how Africa was spelt until the white men came. He asked what we would like our country to be like if we had our way, but gave no one a chance to answer before saying he was sure we would all reply: much cleaner, with wide straight roads all tarred - no potholes - pavements for pedestrians - water flowing in all the taps. No more lights out. No more shanty towns and gutters full of nasty, slimy things. No more mounds of garbage lying around with fat green flies feasting on them. Better health care. More schools, public transport, clean markets, everybody well fed, well dressed and enjoying life, etc. etc. Then he asked what we thought was the reason so many African countries did not have those things. Somebody said, 'Bad government'. Someone else said, 'Too many sinners', to which I could see Solade nodding his head. Khalid muttered, 'It is our fate.' When another person said, 'Because we don't have any ambition,' everybody laughed - that is, everybody except Mr. Azigidah who looked irritated.

He said, 'What are you laughing for? That is the best answer I have heard so far...And why don't we have ambition? ... I shall tell you why. It is because white people have stolen our power from us.'

I would have liked to know how they did that, but he did not explain. He implied that it was something to do with the pyramids, because he then showed us a slide of the back of a one US dollar bill. It had a picture of a pyramid with a flat top and one wide open eye in a triangle above it. The triangle was surrounded by rays of light. Mr

Azigidah said that that single shining eye represents divine power which is what Africans lack. He must have heard the question in all our minds because the next thing he said was, 'Do you know what will give it back to us? … It is by becoming more African, especially where spiritual matters are concerned.'

At that point, I heard chairs scraping the floor and a number of people, Solade among them, got up and walked out, which made Mr. Azigidah so irritated that he threw his arms wide open, exclaiming, 'See what I mean? See what I mean? Brainwashed. There are too many brainwashed Africans around. We New Afrikans believe that God gives every race its own way to harness divine power, and *we* have strayed from our path. No wonder we don't think straight. Our countries will never improve and we shall never be respected in the world until we return to our own spiritual path.'

He got a standing ovation after that, though it was not unanimous. I was one of those whose behinds never left their seats even though the talk had been very interesting. All that stuff about white people stealing our spiritual power sounds too far-fetched to me. And I may be wrong but I don't think it's possible to return to the past either. Our history is our history and we have to move on from there. Khalid agreed with me, but not Chico. *He* joined the long queue when Mr Azigidah asked those who wanted to become New Afrikans to come forward and write their names and addresses in a register. We didn't wait for Chico.

10 February 1996

I am very annoyed with myself because I dreamt about Belinda last night. We were sitting on her steps, kissing and touching each other everywhere. Experienced the usual consequences of lustful dreams. I should have confessed my mortal sin to Father Bassey this evening, but felt too embarrassed. I didn't even go to Confession though I left home for that. This must be how people start backsliding little by little, then stop being Catholics altogether, or else they join other churches where they don't have to make confessions. Mams will be sad if that happens, I know.

I like and respect Mr. Togbah more and more every day. Don't even notice his 'O' legs now. He made me laugh so much today that I had to ask him how he could be so cheerful when he had lost everything. He said, 'My young friend, life belongs to God, so no matter what happens, unless you are going to commit sin by killing yourself, you might as well try to make the best of it. I am not feeling pain anywhere in my body and I have a roof over my head, even though water pours in like morning piss when it rains. I have found a nice young woman to share my pillow and comfort my body and I have work to do that I like and that gives me something in my pocket at the end of the month. After what I have been through, that is enough to make me cheerful. I am only praying for this new war not to come down here.'

Amen.

25 February 1996

No need to look out of my window to see whether it's full moon tonight. Mr. Danso is at it again - *Guide me O Thou Great Jehovah* this time - over and over again and at the top of his voice. I wonder how long he will keep it up this time. It's driving *me* crazy.

A big scare for the Noahs when I was up there this p.m. Mama Abi suddenly collapsed when she was having her evening shower and had to be rushed to hospital. Helped to get her down to the car which wasn't easy because her big body flopped like a puppet on a string. Khalid drove, with Pa Noah beside him and Hamida managed to squeeze herself inside the back to hold her mother's head.

I waited anxiously for them to return. Hamida came up the steps first. She said, 'Manny' in a choked voice and promptly fell into my arms, sobbing. My heart missed a beat because I thought the worst had happened; but it wasn't what I feared, thank God! Pa Noah and Khalid came up after Hamida and said Mama Abi was all right though she had been admitted because her blood pressure was sky high. It must have been relief that made Hamida break down like that. She finally stopped crying, but kept her head against my shoulder for a few moments longer. I felt like pulling her back when she moved away. Strange.

28 February 1996
That Colonel Cobra was back on *Focus on Africa* today, saying that this war is an internal matter and the PRA will not stop attacking the villages up-country until the MRC send all foreign mercenaries away. In the national news bulletin this evening, the MRC spokesman replied, 'No way', regarding the mercenaries and criticised the BBC for continuing to give terrorists 'the oxygen of publicity' (a nice phrase to remember). I was wondering where he got it from when Dad said, 'He is quite right, you know. I remember a BBC news broadcast in the seventies or eighties. Their Prime Minister at the time used those very words when she was talking about their own problems with Irish terrorists.'

3 March 1996
A stranger thing connected with Hamida happened when I was in the queue at the petrol station buying kero this p.m. She came past and told me that Mama Abi had been discharged from hospital. When she gave me the good news her smile lit up her whole face which is perhaps why she suddenly changed before my eyes. It was as if I'd never seen her properly before - her slender neck like those white birds down by the waterside and her skin like a perfect egg plant, so smooth and dark that I felt like stroking it. All of a sudden, I wanted to pull her to me and hold her again - and not in a brotherly way. Very strange!! No wonder Dad is always saying people should expect the unexpected. And how will Khalid take it if I tell him I have fallen for his sister? I won't tell him yet. Perhaps the feelings will go away. But do I want them to? Not sure.

15 March 1996
Mr. Togbah says he is becoming more and more frightened, because more and more people are running away from the fighting up-country. Some have ended up in his refugee camp up the road. He said, 'My young friend, if you see them you will shed tears and curse your fellow human beings. Some of those people have no hands - some, just one foot - some, no ears, some, no lips - all chopped off by PRA fighters. They say some of the PRA fighters are small children, and those ones are even more wicked than the bigger boys. Can you imagine that! *What* is

happening in Africa?'

While he was speaking, he kept punching the mound of dough in front of him as if it were a rebel's body.

Hmm. I'm getting very scared myself. If the fighting comes down here we are finished. Where can we go? Behind us, high hills and thick forest, and the PRA will surely take cover there. In front of us, only the Atlantic Ocean - salt water and sharks.

20 March 1996

Dad asked me to take some provisions for Melvina. I expected the visit to be as strained as before so I asked her grandmother if I could take her out for a walk. A very good idea because once we were outside she began to chat and told me that she would soon be going to join her mother in America. For her sake, I hope that is true, though I would have liked more time to start believing that I have another sister - especially now that I no longer think of Hamida as my little sister. My heart actually jumped when I saw her ahead of us after school. She glanced back when we called out to her, but did not wait. Very disappointed. Doesn't look as if these feelings are going away. Perhaps I should make a move now before someone else 'raids' her.

21 March 1996

Saw amputees with my own eyes this morning when out delivering bread. They were among a big crowd of IDPs carrying clumsy bundles and other things on their heads - all they had managed to bring with them. Poor people. They all looked as if they had trekked for miles. Many of them could hardly walk - their feet were so swollen. I wonder how the ones who have lost one of their feet managed the journey. The faces of all the IDPs looked drained - as if they had been to hell and back. I was so upset, that I couldn't eat anything before going to school. Feelings of impending doom grew even stronger when Jogolo said special prayers for the country at assembly. He asked God to save us from 'demons at play'. So many people sighed deeply that it sounded like the exhalation of a giant.

What with one thing and another, I can't concentrate well

enough to study tonight. Going to bed right now.

30 March 1996

I took the bull by the horns when Khalid and I were strolling home and asked him to fix me up with his sister. He stopped dead to look at me as if I had suddenly grown a second nose.

'You mean Hamida?' he asked - a stupid question - as if he has another sister. '*Copain,* this is sudden-oh.'

I said, 'I know. I was surprised myself. My feelings for her changed just like that.'

To my relief, he began to chuckle as he rubbed his finger and thumb together.

'How much?' he asked. 'I don't do things like that for nothing-oh.'

'*You* are truly a trader's son,' I said, trying to be sarcastic; but that only made him laugh louder and repeat the question. I offered him '*moi-moi*' every day for one month.

'You must be joking!,' he said. 'For my beautiful one and only sister?'

I said, 'Okay, I will give you my shades - the ones Uncle Eku sent from America when I passed GCE.'

Khalid knows I love my shades almost as much as I love my Walkman, so my willingness to give them up really impressed him. He said, 'Wow! you like her that much, eh?'

When I admitted that I did, he added, 'All right - you're my main *copain* after all and I know you will handle my sister with care. Promise me one month's supply of '*moi-moi*' and I will do my best for you.'

I promised readily. I won't go up there again until he gives me her answer. What if she says no? Hmm. I will have to carry on as usual. Nowadays, she hardly ever says anything to me anyway.

3 April 1996

Jogolo has decided that prefects are to lead assembly twice a week 'for your further personal development'. I feel nervous about it, but will do my best when the time comes.

It's four days since I spoke to Khalid about Hamida. He keeps saying, '*Copain*, be patient, be patient, you know my sister is not an easy person these days.'

I asked him how she answered when he gave her the message and he told me she said, 'I have heard.'

I asked him how she looked and he said, 'She just smiled.'

Hmm. Was that a hopeful sign? Mams, of course, has guessed that something is up. I'm glad she didn't press me when I told her it was nothing. The lines on her forehead have returned - even more noticeably than before. It must be because of her quarrel with Dad and the sight of all those amputees.

Confided in Mr. Togbah about my situation regarding Hamida. He said, 'My young friend, haven't you heard that it is the patient dog that gets the best bone?'

Patience again. Always patience. Patience has never been one of Emmanuel's virtues. In any case, I don't care if Hamida isn't the best bone. She is the bone I want.

10 April 1996

Rumours, rumours, rumours. People are now saying that the MRC have agreed to send Security Solutions away. I hope to God that is true because, it seems as if all hell has broken loose up-country - literally. Jogolo prayed for us to be saved from demons at play but the things that are happening these days make me tremble. I think what we should be praying for is be to be saved from demons that have cut loose. No one can tell me that this is still about saving the country. Something else is going on. Something really nasty. Solade says it is spiritual warfare and quoted a Bible passage about principalities and powers. I don't understand any of that. All *I* know is that now my blood runs cold whenever I think about the PRA.

18 April 1996

My best birthday present ever. Hamida's answer at last. A short note and a beautiful photo of herself: 'Dear Manny, okay. Hamida.' It's the first time I've seen her hand-writing - so neat and even, every letter clearly formed. Something else to admire about her. Absolutely delighted, but now I have to work out how we are going to spend time alone together like a boyfriend and girlfriend. Pa Noah and Mama Abi watch her like hawks.

20 April 1996

It seems that the rumours were true. The PRA have announced the end of 'Operation no mercy' and a ceasefire. Hope that means the streams of IDPs and amputees will start drying up now. How can human beings behave like that to other human beings? Sewa City is now bursting with IDPs. I was jostled on the pavement several times today. Overpowering body odours and even higher mountains of garbage everywhere. Came home early, very bad-tempered and needing a second bath. More annoyed because that meant another trip to the waterside.

Up to the Noahs later - my first meeting with Hamida since she agreed to become my girlfriend. I thought the visit would be a bit strained because Khalid kept his distance; but it was okay after the first few minutes. Even though Khalid had told me a lot about their trip, to break the ice, I asked her what she had liked best about London. Her eyes lit up. She said, 'I liked *everything*,' and promptly began a non-stop description of underground trains, moving staircases that are called escalators, double-decker buses, enormous shops and supermarkets and other wonderful things. She told me something I hadn't heard from Khalid - that they even have supermarkets for pet animals!! Imagine! Just as she used to, she kept me so entertained with her chatting that I'm now wondering whether her silence before had something to do with me. A question to be asked and answered one day soon.

Khalid walked me halfway down the hill afterwards and together we solved the problem of 'time alone together.' Next weekend, we shall ask to go to a film at Orion - he and Melrose, Hamida and me. We don't think Pa Noah and Mama Abi will object to that. I'll also start going to the BC library at least once a week and ask Hamida to do the same.

30 June 1996

Took assembly again. My hands still shake a bit at the start but I am enjoying being on the stage in a position of authority and leading the singing. I felt wonderful when Mammy B commended my performance. Her cheeks seem almost normal these days. I hope that means she's getting better.

Heavy downpour. Lights out again, so early to bed.

25 September 1996
A happy, happy day. Only two things prevented it from being perfect - the cold war at home and the hot war in the country. To the BC library this a.m. after my usual chores. Hamida joined me later. We spent two hours reading quietly together, exchanging glances and smiles now and then, and touching fingertips! Absolute bliss! Things began to happen, but felt no embarrassment because the table hid my bottom half and it did not last. Strolled home together afterwards - slowly - to prolong the pleasure, talking all the way. Back to British Council this evening to see Wole Soyinka play *Trials of Brother Jero* put on by University Dramatic Society. Pa Noah allowed Khalid to take his car, which was great. Thoroughly enjoyed the performance, especially watching it with my darling's hand in mine. How we laughed! Afterwards, we dropped Melrose at her house before going home. Khalid escorted her to the door and the moment they left, Hamida and I fell into each other's arms, laughing again. Our lips met and clung together like magnets. Things happened so strongly that for a while I thought I would explode. I'm becoming more and more crazy about that girl. Won't allow even water to come between us. Ever. I shall write and tell her so right now.

Chapter Eleven

THE PRA TRIUMPHS AGAIN

Ever since the BBC's *'Focus on Africa'* programme came on air, Kanekeh had been waiting for a report on the latest developments in the war. It had been pushed off the headlines by other news - the growing concern over the spread of AIDS in southern Africa, and a ferry disaster somewhere else which had killed more than three hundred people. The report on his war came only during the last ten minutes of the programme; but it was well worth the delay. As he had predicted, under pressure from the big international powers, the MRC government had decided to break their contract with the white mercenaries in order to end the terrible suffering of helpless villagers up-country and were now willing to negotiate a truce with the PRA.

Kanekeh laughed out loud on hearing this, slapping his thigh with glee. He was still grinning broadly as he switched off his radio and strode out to the porch to summon the commanders.

'What did I tell you?' he bragged, chuckling into his beard as he passed on the good news. 'Operation no mercy' has done its work… 'Operation no mercy' has done its work. You see what I told you? Once you know people's psychology, you can make things happen the way you want them to. It's all the same whether you are dealing with governments or the United Nations. They are all made up of people, and people are people. Remember that - you might find it useful one day… O, this is so wonderful!'

He sprang to his feet, rubbing his hands together the way he did before attacking his food.

'Let us pray,' he declared, 'And standing up this time…Almighty God/Allah, we praise your holy name for helping us to achieve this goal. Do help us now to continue this struggle with even greater zeal, so that all the people of this country can enjoy the kind of life they deserve. Amen.'

Kanekeh now proceeded to outline his next moves towards dealing with the military government. Still full of his triumph, he had not noticed the glances Cobra and Leopard exchanged during his boasting.

The two commanders excluded from 'Operation no mercy' had talked a good deal about their concern that Kanekeh seemed so ready to abandon ideals he once preached, and they found the contrast between their leader before his last trip across the border and the present Kanekeh even more disturbing after the first raid in connection with 'Operation no mercy.' When L-C Odinga showed them shocking trophies - two bloody right hands severed at the wrist, Kanekeh barely glanced at them before saying, 'Well done...Keep it up.'

While they appreciated the need to end the menace of the helicopter gunships, Cobra and Leopard loathed the idea of using terror tactics against harmless villagers. Apart from these scruples, they also feared that such tactics would fatally damage the campaign which had begun with such noble ideals. Who would trust the PRA to govern the country after such unwarranted cruelty towards the very people they were supposed to be saving from oppression and injustice? How could Kanekeh be so unconcerned about this danger, they wondered. In the end, agreeing that they could not continue to support a leader who encouraged terror tactics, they decided to wait and see how the situation unfolded after the current operation, before deciding what to do.

By this time, Colonel Cobra, being the most well-spoken of the commanders, was once again in good standing with their leader, for no sooner had the MRC reacted to 'Operation no mercy' on the air waves, than Kanekeh had asked him to act as PRA spokesman. It was Cobra who had made clear to the MRC, the reasons for the PRA's campaign of terror and the conditions for ending it.

'Contact them via the BBC and set up a meeting to say that we accept the truce,' Kanekeh now instructed him. 'Meanwhile, Major Leopard, I want you and your boys to find out the positions of the government soldiers around the diamond fields so that I can decide what strategy to use for dealing with them. Report back to me as soon as possible. Cobra, get Mamba on the radio. I want all remaining commanders here for a war council in three days' time. Dismissed.'

<><><><><>

Samu almost jumped for joy when Major Leopard informed him that they would be going on a reconnaissance mission. Relief was, however, the stronger emotion, because though 'Operation no mercy' now seemed to be over, his longing to escape from the PRA had grown stronger in the past weeks. Events at Camp Freedom had contributed to his deepening unhappiness - the sight of Odinga all puffed up, strutting around after Kanekeh promoted him to the rank of Colonel, new groups of miserable conscripts having to submit to the ordeal of branding, and worst of all, his sister, Mawa walking in a funny round-shouldered way, trying to hide the small bulge which was changing the shape of her waist. She avoided him altogether these days, averting her eyes if she saw him approaching, and scurrying away like a little rat whenever he tried to talk to her. Major Leopard had told himself and Lans, the other person chosen for the reconnaissance detail, that they would be going into dangerous territory for about a month. In spite of the anxiety this information aroused, Samu still preferred going on a risky mission to remaining in Camp Freedom.

They set out the very next day, travelling in a north-westerly direction. In this part of the forest, the lofty trees grew so close together that their luxuriant foliage formed a canopy which looked impenetrable from above though a certain amount of dappled sunlight filtered through unseen gaps in the leaves. The forest floor was, however, surprisingly free from heavy undergrowth which made their progress more rapid than might have been expected. It also helped that Major Leopard obviously knew exactly where they were going.

Leopard used the opportunity offered by their journey, to improve both their tracking skills and their ability to survive in the forest. For the second time since his conscription into the PRA, Samu almost felt like an ordinary boy again, and nothing made him happier than earning the praise of his hero. He readily undertook and easily passed the little tests Leopard set for himself and Lans as they made their way through the forest. Impressed by Samu's growing skills and eagerness to do well , the commander began to refer to him fondly as 'Small Leopard' unaware that Lans, thinking Samu a threat to his place on the training team, had become jealous of the talented newcomer. Since they always walked in single file with Leopard well in the lead, Lans now began to find subtle ways of irritating Samu without the leader's knowledge. On one occasion, he put a foot out to trip the boy, on another, he allowed an overhanging branch to slap him in the face and on yet another, jostled him just as he was about to put a piece of raw cassava into his mouth, so that the morsel fell to the ground. As usual, Lans offered an apology which Samu accepted. After a few more of these 'accidents' Samu began to suspect Lans of deliberately causing them. However, to keep the peace, he continued to ignore the provocation until the day his companion stepped over a Gabon viper, lying half concealed by fallen leaves and failed to alert him to the danger. Samu detected a movement under the leaves only seconds before his foot would have come down on the deadly snake.

Each member of the spy party was carrying a cutlass to clear a path through the tangled vegetation if necessary, and also for just such an emergency; so Samu coolly dealt the slow-moving snake a fatal blow. He might have continued to keep his suspicions to himself, had Lans resisted the temptation to gloat. Lans did not. Instead, he turned around with such a malicious grin that, muttering a curse, Samu picked up the dead snake and flung it in his direction. The heavy carcass landed on the side of Lans's neck, almost knocking him over. No sooner did he regain his balance than he sprang on the younger boy, sending them both crashing to the forest floor. Being the stronger of the two by far, Lans had landed two punishing blows against Samu's head before the sound of grunts and violent movements sent Leopard rushing back to see what was happening.

'What am I seeing?' the commander hissed, his eyes darting from one combatant to the other like flashing lights. He slapped them about the ears as he pulled them apart. 'Do you want to kill us all? Don't you realize you could betray our whereabouts to the enemy with all this noise? Lans, *you* are the elder and more experienced. You should know better. And what are you fighting about anyway?'

'I nearly stepped on that very bad snake because of him, sah,' Samu replied still panting from exertion and rage as he pointed to the carcass of the Gabon viper. 'And this is not the first time. He has been doing all kinds of things to annoy me, like…'

'Why?' Leopard demanded of Lans, glaring, without waiting for Samu to list any other misdeeds.

Lans did not reply. Instead, shifting dead leaves and twigs under his feet with the toe of one filthy canvas shoe, he hung his head sulkily. Only then did Leopard suspect jealousy to be the reason for his behaviour and try to destroy *that* deadly plant before it took deeper root.

'Come over here and sit down, both of you,' he ordered, leading the boys to a flattish, moss-covered boulder he had noticed in passing.

With a degree of sternness the boys never would have guessed the commander possessed, Leopard started talking about the importance of their present assignment, reminding them of the reasons for which the PRA was fighting a war. It was in the course of admonishing the boys that he realized how much he had himself embraced the ideals of the movement and disliked the new direction it seemed to be taking. Let God not agree to that, he prayed silently while telling his younger comrades in arms that if *they* fought each other, the PRA would not be strong enough to fight its enemies.

'We are fighting for a good cause,' he said. 'Do you want the PRA to fail?'

Had he chosen to give an honest answer, Samu would have said that, except in so far as the outcome of the war might affect his future, he could not care less who won it. However, he gave the answer he knew would best please his hero. Lans gave Leopard a similar assurance that he did not want them to lose the war, though in his case, the answer was perfectly sincere. He had joined the PRA of his own accord, persuaded to do so by Kanekeh himself.

'So… we are going to support each other, from now on, not so?' Leopard asked, throwing each one a significant glance as he rose to continue their journey.

'Yessah,' the boys replied, looking somewhat ashamed of themselves. Lans, however, continued to regard Samu as a rival, though he pretended otherwise and gave him no further cause for complaint.

Later that day, they emerged into thick bush which, though much less awe-inspiring than the rain forest, nevertheless made their journey more difficult on account of the shoulder high grass through which they had to force their way. It was not until the late afternoon of the following day that they came to an open plain overlooking a river valley. Down below was the town of Dembu the district headquarters and centre of the diamond trade.

To the left of the town's perimeter they saw a vast fenced in area which Leopard told them was probably the concession the MRC had given to the white mercenaries who had almost succeeded in wiping out the PRA - Security Solutions, they were called. Beyond the fence they saw huge heaps of dirt like so many giant ant hills set close together. A little below them flowed the Dembu River on whose banks the spies made out hundreds of men, most of them bent double as they searched for diamonds in muddy craters.

The first sight of Dembu left Samu slack-jawed with amazement. Never had he seen so many large concrete buildings, most of them with roofs of corrugated iron, even if the roofs were stained with rust, or so many people of every description. And shops upon shops - some selling bread, others second-hand clothes, others an astonishing variety of items from lanterns to packets of sugar. The most common items on sale seemed to be head pans, sieves, shovels and pick-axes - the equipment of diamond diggers, Leopard explained. Almost everything in sight seemed to be covered in dust - buildings people, trees, animals, as well as the various vehicles rocking and lurching as they picked their way along the badly rutted road. The vehicles were the greatest wonder to Samu who, before the PRA rebels came, had never left his village and had therefore never seen such marvels.

'The first thing we must do,' Leopard told them, 'is to find work as diamond diggers. Small Leopard, on no account are you to remove your shirt, you hear me? Otherwise you will give yourself away. And don't get into any fights, because someone might pull it off. We have to go softly, softly and not draw attention to ourselves. Talk as little as possible. Just look and listen, you hear?'

They were surprised at the lack of checkpoints which allowed them to drift through the town unchallenged. The reason for this carelessness was explained when they discovered that most of the soldiers stationed in Dembu spent the best part of the day either digging for diamonds or else washing gravel for the officers in command. They only returned to barracks and military discipline in the evenings. From conversations Leopard and the two young spies overheard when they joined the mining crews, it also became clear that despite the imminent departure of the mercenaries the diamond fields were not considered in danger of an attack from the decimated rebel army.

‘I think it will be easy to take them back,’ once those mercenaries have gone, Papa,’ Leopard reported to Kanekeh on their return a month later.

‘In that case,’ said the wily Kanekeh, we shall pretend that our interests lie elsewhere in the country for the time being, then attack them during the day and with full force.’

<><><><><>

As the three spies re-entered the camp they heard screams coming from Colonel Odinga’s quarters. Fearing the worst, heart racing, Samu broke away from his companions and ran towards the sound. Without stopping to consider the consequences of entering without the owner’s permission, he burst unceremoniously into the little shack. Fortunately for him, Odinga was nowhere to be seen. Only Kanekeh’s woman was visible. On seeing Samu, she made urgent gestures for him to remain outside, whispering, ‘This is not a place for you.’

But he brushed past her and fell to his knees beside the mat where his sister lay. The metallic smell of blood rose from Mawa’s body as she writhed and screamed, calling for her mother, then becoming aware of Samu‘s presence pleading in a heartbreaking whimper for him to help her.

‘What is happening?’ he demanded of Kanekeh’s woman.

Avoiding his frightened eyes, she answered with an air of mystery, ‘Water is wasting. Don’t worry. Sometimes these things happen. Your sister will be all right once she is empty again. I know what to do.’

None the wiser as to the cause of Mawa’s illness but suspecting that it had something to do with her swelling belly, Samu cursed Odinga under his breath. He cursed him more fiercely when, two days later, Kanekeh's woman told him with an air of alarm, that Mawa's belly had become as tight as a drum and abnormally swollen; and her whole body was burning with fever.

'I am doing my best for her, but she should be in a hospital,' she added, shaking her head in a way that told Samu her best might not be enough to save his sister's life. 'I will beg Colonel Odinga to allow you to come and see her for a few minutes every day.'

Barely a week after that warning, Samu and other junior fighters were practising assembly/disassembly skills and cleaning their AK-47s, when Colonel Odinga came striding towards them. Addressing Samu without the slightest expression of regret in word or look, he said,'Come and take your sister. She has died in my place.'

As if she was only a dog, Samu thought, staring at the commander with undisguised loathing. As Odinga made to move away, Samu sprang at him in mindless rage causing his horrified companions to drop the metal pieces they were cleaning and jump to their feet intent on preventing an assault whose consequences were bound to be terrible. Their intervention proved unnecessary, however, for Colonel Odinga merely flicked his fingers at Samu's forehead and pushed him away, saying, 'Have you forgotten this, or do you want me to give you something else to remember me by? Just do as you told and don't annoy me.'

He strode away leaving Samu so enraged that he would have gone for Odinga a second time, had not his companions firmly held him back.

'Leave that one to God', they said, trying to calm him down. 'Let us go. We will help you to carry her.'

But for their frequent words of sympathy urging caution, Samu might have made yet another reckless attempt to avenge Mawa's death. Instead, another ball of anger stayed locked in his heart like a trapped lion awaiting an opportunity to go for a throat - any throat, if he could not sink his teeth into the one he wanted.

<><><><><><>

Kanekeh's plan for retaking the diamond fields might have failed had the PRA faced an enemy determined to prevent them doing so. As it happened, retaking Dembu was accomplished with little loss of life on either side.

Almost as soon as news came on the radio that the last helicopter gunship had departed, Cobra, Leopard, Rambo and Pele, the commanders Kanekeh ordered to retake the diamond fields, started making their way to Dembu with their fighters. They arrived there at dawn and had stealthily surrounded the town by the time the miner/soldiers began their daily activity of digging and washing diamond-carrying gravel. Firing rapid sequential rounds to deceive the town as to their numbers, the attacking force achieved total surprise and caused panic among the miner/soldiers, who promptly dropped their sieves, shovels and head pans and fled in the direction of the bush from which the PRA fighters had earlier emerged. Meanwhile, in Dembu itself, after a half-hearted attempt to repel the attack resulted in the loss of a dozen men, including his deputy, the commanding officer, raised a white flag of truce in the forlorn hope that it would prevent the rest of them from being slaughtered. The PRA fighters maintained their offensive positions, but stopped firing at once, following Kanekeh's orders that the objective of this operation was not only to recapture the diamond fields but also to expand the PRA, if possible, by offering the government soldiers an opportunity to change sides.

Colonel Cobra and his fellow commanders made the pre-arranged proposal:

'Surrender and agree to fight on the side of the PRA and you can continue digging diamonds with us. Our leader will control all mining in the area, but you will receive your fair share. If you refuse, we shall have no alternative but to attack again and fight you to the end. You have twenty-four hours to make up your minds.'

Though he knew it would cost him his life, the commanding officer treated the proposal with the contempt he felt it deserved.

'No need to wait till tomorrow,' he said. 'Do you think all of us are the same? People without morals? I prefer to die than to fight beside mad dogs like you people.'

'All right, you had your chance,' Cobra said, raising his hand, though he did so with a feeling of regret that he was ordering the death of a man worthy of respect.

Having earlier taken up a sniping position in a breadfruit tree, with his rifle pointing straight at the camp commander's head, Pele had been waiting for the signal to shoot him down. On seeing Cobra's raised hand, he squeezed the trigger. As the commander fell, Cobra repeated the offer and was relieved when the rest of the government soldiers in the vicinity, accepted the terms of the surrender. Once the ammunition dump and weapons store had been secured, he triumphantly radioed Camp Freedom with the news that the PRA was once again in full control of Dembu.

'A great victory for us! Congrats.' Kanekeh shouted into the receiver. 'You are all promoted with immediate effect. From today, you are Brigadier Cobra, Pele is Colonel, Leopard is Lieutenant-Colonel and Rambo becomes a Major. Over.'

'Thank you, Papa,' Cobra said. 'I shall tell them. Over.'

'The next thing is for me to move my headquarters to Dembu. Find a suitable place for my personal quarters, then send transport to take me there. It is to come as close to this place as possible. Is that clear? Over.'

'Yes, Papa. Over.'

'All right. I am waiting,' Kanekeh told him. 'Over and out.'

Within a few days, Camp Freedom was deserted. The other commanders travelled to Dembu by the mini-van commandeered to transport Kanekeh, his woman and their household goods while the rest of the fighters made their way there on foot. Unlike similar journeys in the past, this one proceeded in a relaxed atmosphere since the area no longer harboured any enemies the PRA feared.

<><><><><>

Dembu was the perfect location for the PRA's headquarters for it boasted an airstrip in reasonable condition which greatly simplified the procurement of supplies. Flying in and out at will on a small plane, Malick resumed a brisk trade in arms in exchange for diamonds. He was also mining on his own account again, in the large area allocated to him by courtesy of Kanekeh. After months of wondering whether his hopes of increasing his wealth from this source would have to be abandoned for good, he was once again feeling satisfied with the progress of their venture.

Gradually word reached the fugitive miner/soldiers that they had nothing to fear if they agreed to fight for the PRA instead of the government. To their credit, some of the soldiers rejected the offer, preferring to seek out their comrades stationed in other parts of the country, and who had remained loyal to the government. For the majority, however, the lure of diamonds proved stronger than any loyalty to the MRC government. Only too willing to pledge allegiance to the PRA, they returned to Dembu where they were joined by other young people ready to stake their future on Kanekeh's success.

The rainy season which had started just as the PRA returned to Dembu now settled in and in order to strengthen the loyalty of these new recruits, Kanekeh used the wet months to indoctrinate them on the purpose and ideals of the PRA. Since none of the new recruits could deny that most citizens of the country had been failed by one government after another, it was not difficult to win their hearts and minds. By the time the last thunderstorms had passed over Dembu, Kanekeh had become confident enough in their loyalty to call a council of war to make plans for a push towards the capital. It would be another operation requiring iron nerves and a complete lack of conscience on the part of the commanders in charge. He therefore chose Colonel Odinga, to lead the expedition, supported by Mamba, Pele and Ironbone. Instead of L-C Leopard, he put Rambo in charge of reconnaissance.

Chapter Twelve

LIGHTNING AND THUNDER

2 October 1996

My first full shave today. Managed to cut myself in the process. Glad there was no comment from Dad though he must have noticed the little piece of toilet roll I put on my chin to absorb the blood. He has more important things on his mind these days - like everyone else. The PRA have started gaining ground again. The latest rumour is that many of our soldiers are now fighting alongside the rebels, pretending to be loyal soldiers during the day and joining PRA raids at night. No wonder the PRA are always ambushing our troops or taking them by surprise. What a betrayal!!! And to think those turncoat soldiers are the people supposed to be protecting us!

19 October 1996

The news is getting worse by the day. All resistance to the PRA has now crumbled and they have over-run the diamond fields again. Not surprising after so many desertions to them by government soldiers. To date, as many as one thousand, people say. The soldier traitors are no longer even pretending to be loyal, and no doubt, the PRA will get even more recruits now that they hold the winning cards - the diamond fields. I am surprised, though very relieved that there is still no general call-up. Trying to prepare my mind for the possibility, but it is hard. I, for one, don't feel any loyalty to this government. They are no better than the previous one after all. We have never been made to feel that we have a stake in this country, so what would I be fighting for? Ordinary people don't seem to matter. Is that how a country should be?

10 December 1996

More rumours today - that there is finally going to be a military call-up for all able-bodied men aged between 17 and 35. People are saying that some of the rich high-ups have already started sending their sons abroad. Hmm. Emmanuel, get ready-oh. People like you will have no choice if it really happens. I wonder whether Pa Noah will send Khalid away. Somehow, I doubt it. He's not the type. On the other hand, perhaps for Mama Abi's sake, because anxiety is bad for her. But will my *copain* agree to go? That is the question. I'll ask him tomorrow.

11 December 1996

Khalid says that if they try to make him leave the country, he will threaten to leave home. So relieved to hear that, that I felt like kneeling before him in gratitude. I know I'm being selfish, but I can't help it. I always feel better when Khalid is around.

26 January 1997

Every day now there are fresh rumours going round and round like bats at sunset. Dad came home with the latest and most alarming one so far - that the PRA are here - hiding in the forest reserve, getting ready to attack the capital. How do people know these things? Or is it that PRA agents are the very ones spreading the rumours to scare us. This p.m. Pa Noah sent Khalid and me round George Town to summon all heads of households to a meeting at his house on Thursday. He says the time has come to think the unthinkable - what to do if the rebels come down to this province and attack Sewa City.

30 January 1997

Hamida's fifteenth birthday. Gave her a handkerchief with blue lace round it - all I could afford. Walked up to their house with Dad when he was going to the meeting and stayed in the yard with Khalid till I asked him to call Hamida. She joined me without Mama Abi knowing and we were able to forget about the war and everything else for about fifteen minutes before Khalid returned to say Mama Abi needed her upstairs. It was much too soon. Hamida let me touch her soft breast through her blouse - a sweet sensation which I can't wait to experience again.

There were noisy discussions in the house. Dad later reported to us (Gramma Cobola included, because she wasn't able to climb the hill).

A) As from today, we should all consider ourselves on sentry duty.

B) By tomorrow all households are to choose a hiding place (obviously the wood store for us), and start storing dry food there (cabin bread biscuits, *garri*), and tinned food (sardines, corned beef, luncheon meat, tinned milk) and any spare cash. Also water, though that is a problem. How long will it stay fresh?

C) Anyone who hears unusual movements or sounds in the night should raise the alarm by banging pots and pans, the way some people carry on when there is an eclipse of the moon.

Dad looked a bit embarrassed telling us about C), but even if we feel foolish banging pans together, it will be a good way to give people time to take cover. He also told us that the Hunting Society announced that they are going to form a militia, like some towns up-country have started doing. I asked what use those ancient guns of theirs would be against AK-47s and RPGs. Apparently, it's a matter of pride and dignity. They prefer to meet death fighting like men that to wait for it like sheep.

2 February 1997

All is quiet - more so than usual, but there are still plenty of rumours that the PRA are here already, and also that all the foreign embassies are evacuating their people. Mams looks worried all the time now and Dad keeps his radio on all night in case there is an announcement that needs instant action. Everybody looks tired, because nobody is sleeping well. Not much laughter or even conversation. Plenty of heavy sighs. Khalid and Hamida are very worried about Mama Abi again. This tension is too much for her. Hmm.

16 February 1997

Helped in 'Millie's Corner' until 9 o'clock. These days Dad's customers glance around before speaking and barely open their mouths when they do. Hmm. When I remember how loud and lively they used to be… Fear is powerful-oh.

17 February 1997

The Information Secretary made a statement on the radio after the 6 o'clock news, saying the situation in the country is serious, but that those of us living in and around the capital should not believe the rumours circulating about the PRA being close at hand. He said, 'First of all, according to our intelligence, the rumours are unfounded, and secondly, government is expecting troops from a friendly neighbouring country to come to our aid very soon. They will assist loyal soldiers to fight off the PRA gangsters trying to destroy our beloved country.'

Somehow the statement did nothing to lessen our anxiety. When he finished, Mams sucked her teeth loudly and walked away. Dad said, 'Things are getting out of hand. That should be plain to anyone with any sense. Government officials never tell the truth at times like this.'

I must remember to put all my diaries in a plastic bag and take them down to the store otherwise I shall surely forget them if we have to move in a hurry. I wouldn't like to lose them at all.

23 February 1997

A procession of mighty khaki-coloured lorries emerged from the road to the airport when Khalid and I were on our way to school this a.m. Some of them turned right and drove towards the city. Some turned left, heading up-country - all of them crammed full of soldiers armed to the teeth. They looked tougher than our own soldiers somehow. Perhaps because they were generally darker and some of them had scars on their cheeks as if they had been slashed with knives. We waited to see what else had come. There were armoured vehicles - at least a dozen of them, all with mounted guns, then truckload after truckload of machine guns, rocket launchers, RPGs, and other fearsome weapons we couldn't identify. Khalid and I found the sight of them so exciting that we joined other passers-by waving at the procession and calling out, 'Thank you…thank you' and 'Welcome…welcome.' Then we looked at each other and said, 'Wow!'

Another day when I simply couldn't concentrate. Excitement and fear all rolled into one. What next?

Chapter Thirteen

SPIES IN SEWA CITY

If his first sight of Dembu left Samu open-mouthed with wonder, his first experience of Sewa City almost struck him dumb. For several days he hardly spoke, as his mind strove to comprehend the vastness of the place - buildings with several storeys, some as high as ten or twelve, and of enormous dimensions. Then there were the many roads flowing into one another like motionless rivers, most of them covered with some dark substance which concealed the earth beneath. Moving ceaselessly up and down these bewildering thoroughfares were vehicles of many colours, sizes and shapes, as well as hundreds of people, some going up and down with an appearance of purpose, while others strolled aimlessly about as if they had nothing to do or were hardly aware of their surroundings. And the noise was deafening - a steady hum of human voices frequently interrupted by blasts from the horns of passing vehicles.

Mingling in the crowds with his comrades, Samu looked and marvelled, looked and marvelled, almost forgetting in his fascination, that they were there to prepare for an attack. And he was not the only one; with the result that although they were dressed in T-shirts, old jeans and battered canvas shoes or plastic slippers like many other youths their age, during their first day in the city, so many curious eyes glanced their way that when they returned to their hideout in the forest reserve Colonel Pele and Major Rambo, commanders of the advance party, decided that only the small number of fighters familiar with the larger up-country towns would be used to reconnoitre the city. They ordered the rest to stay well out of sight and concentrate on locating other hideouts as well as escape routes.

Sent by Major Rambo to reconnoitre the city's westernmost areas, Lans and Samu finally found themselves on a grassy ridge facing the distant ocean. Coming from a the part of the country in which there were only rivers and not particularly wide ones at that, their first sight of that vast expanse of shimmering, grey-green water had filled the boys with as much awe and wonder as the man-made marvels which had taken their breath away in the city centre. However, the ocean was not what was holding their attention at the present time. They were surveying a huge, beautifully clean compound fenced all the way around with wire mesh. It lay between the ridge on which they were sitting and the sea, and contained six of the strangest buildings they had ever set eyes on - all of them identical, long and low to the ground. The boys could not tell where the walls ended and the roofs began because the buildings seemed to be constructed from long, curved corrugated iron sheets painted dark grey. They looked like enormous kerosene drums cut in half, lengthwise. Three windows had been cut into the metal walls. They noticed people - adults and boys of various ages - going in and out at both ends and concluded rightly that the buildings had front and back entrances.

'What kind of place is this?' Lans wondered aloud. 'A school?'

'Perhaps.' said Samu. 'The boys have on uniforms...'

As they continued their secret surveillance, a lorry drove up to the gates of the compound and six boys and two adults alighted - government soldiers, judging from their combat uniforms.

From their hiding place, Lans and Samu, now watched events unfold with growing fascination. The soldiers had a word with the guards at the gate, then proceeded to the building nearest to it. They stood outside for a minute or so before an elderly white man came out to greet them. He put an arm round the shoulders of two of the new arrivals, obviously saying something to them, while the soldiers returned to the lorry and brought out a number of guns and cartridge belts which they took to the far side of the compound and flung to the ground in a heap. Next, the white man called out to someone inside the office and another man, this time a well-built African, emerged. He went to the other five buildings one at a time and within a few minutes about thirty other boys and a few more adults came outside. They grouped themselves with the new arrivals near the first building. One of the soldiers bent down to the pile of weaponry, then rapidly straightened up and backed away. Not a moment too soon, it turned out, because flames suddenly shot towards the sky and cartridges started exploding like gunshots. The assembled boys and adults clapped, cheered and began to sing:

'No more, no more
We are not fighting any more;
No more, no more
We are not fighting any more.
Guns are gone,
Bullets gone.
We are not fighting any more;
No more, no more, no more.'
WE WANT PEACE!'

'O...O...,' Lans said, as understanding dawned. 'This is one of those camps they were talking about on the radio the other day. Do you remember?'

The turncoat soldiers among the PRA fighters had brought their few valuables with them, including radios which now served the dual purpose of keeping all the fighters hiding out in the forest reserve up to date with news of the progress of the war elsewhere, and lessening their boredom as they awaited orders. Lans was referring to a vernacular news broadcast which they had listened to a few nights before setting out on their present mission. It had mentioned attempts by the government to woo child soldiers back to normal life. The PRA audience had greeted this idea with laughter and derisive comments.

'Look at the cowards,' Lans now muttered scornfully as the new boys were led to another of the buildings. 'They are going to tell those people all our secrets... Colonel Odinga should blast this place when we attack the capital.'

'Perhaps they were caught,' Samu suggested, gazing with intense longing at the scene below them. 'Or perhaps they just became tired of fighting. Don't you ever feel that way?'

'Never,' Lans replied and promptly started to sing the PRA anthem - quietly but with all the passion of a fanatic.

'Don't you get tired of seeing blood?' Samu asked.

Lans's forehead creased with annoyance.

'Look,' he said. 'You cannot have rice to eat without brushing and burning the ground. That is all there is to it, as far as I am concerned. The PRA has work to do. We fighters should not even think of giving up until it is finished. Let us go.'

After that Samu held his tongue, but he could not help throwing backward glances towards the camp as they rose to retrace their steps. After all the danger, deprivation and harshness of his present existence, the scene below beckoned like a gentle voice calling out, 'Samu, come and join us. Come and join us.'

Lans noticed his backward glances, and urged him in a harsher tone, 'Let us *go*. Or are you also thinking about giving up the fight?'

Samu hurriedly assured him that that was not the case, but for days afterwards, he kept remembering that compelling scene, even as the rest of the PRA forces joined them and the final preparations to seize the capital got under way.

Chapter Fourteen

THE DELUGE

15-20 May 1997 (what happened between 27 February and 13 March)

It's now ten days since I came back to George Town. Gramma Cobola's chin is resting on her chest and she's snoring away like an old engine. I don't know if I'll be able to concentrate with the noise she's making but, though the pen still feels heavy in my hand, I feel capable of beginning to record the story of my life as it has unfolded in the last three months.

The arrival of the foreign troops gave us a degree of confidence in the Information Secretary's assurances, but as things turned out, help had arrived far too late. The foreign soldiers must barely have had time to unpack their gear and set up their tents before the PRA struck.

They came around midnight. Rather, they attacked Sewa City around midnight, because it turned out that all those rumours were well founded after all - once again, the common saying that there's no smoke without a fire proved to be true. PRA fighters had secretly entered the capital by pretending to be civilians fleeing the fighting up-country and had already established themselves in the hills overlooking the capital, while the MRC were taking their desperate last minute measures to save the capital.

Piecing together the events of that night, I have come to the conclusion that there were two signals given. The first was the sudden burst of gunfire we heard coming from somewhere to the east of George Town around midnight. The dogs began to bark as frantically as if one of them had caught sight of a black mamba, and we leapt out of bed. No lights as usual. All three of us collided in the inky darkness. Even though I hadn't been running, I felt out of breath, my heart thumping. Typically, Mams said, 'Let us pray,' but even *she* could find no words except 'Holy Mary mother of God, pray for us sinners,' which she kept on repeating and repeating under her breath. The effect was the opposite of calming, especially since every few seconds, more gunfire exploded. The blasts seemed to be coming closer and in the short intervals between eruptions, we became aware of an uproar in the distance. It was difficult to explain it at first, but as the noise increased, we realised that what we were hearing were desperate cries, stampeding feet, and vehicles honking their horns, stopping, starting, crashing gears and accelerating abruptly. Added to this confusion of sounds was singing - a kind of victory chant sung loudly enough to burst the singers' vocal cords. That triumphant chorus must have been the second signal because amid the frantic barking of the dogs, we now heard another more terrifying sound. It was the same boastful singing, but this time approaching George Town itself from the forest reserve behind the village, and growing louder by the minute. Very soon, we began to hear the words of the song which were:

The PRA is fighting to save our motherland.
The PRA is fighting to save our motherland.
The people will have food again,
The country will be saved.
The people will find work again.
The country will be saved.
The people will have health again.
The country will be saved.
POWER TO THE PEOPLE!'

'Lord, have mercy,' Mams muttered. 'You people, hurry up, hurry up.'

Within two minutes we had rushed down the back steps according to plan, and scrambled into the pitch-black, damp-smelling store beneath the house. Dad came clutching his radio and Mams, two bottles of water and her rosary. I took my most precious possessions - my Walkman and diary with Hamida's photo hidden in it. We sat on the thin latex foam mattresses Dad had bought just the week before and waited fearfully. Mams stifled a cry as something, probably a rat, ran over her foot.

Down the potholed street came a rowdy gang of PRA thugs. After the song, they started chanting obscene insults and threats which made me break out in a sweat though the night was cool.

'Just you wait,' they jeered in their coarse voices. 'We are coming to deal with you people who think you are too good to join the PRA and fight for your country. Just you wait. All these houses are coming down. Just you wait'

They banged on doors and rattled metal gates as they passed. A rapid burst of gunfire and a wailing howl told us they had aimed shots at the dogs and hit at least one of them. Expecting the door of our hiding place to crash open any minute, I almost wet myself with fear. However, their chanting, shouting, cursing, banging and crazy shooting gradually faded away and we breathed normally again.

<><><><><>

After so many days of the radio being on all night, the power in Dad's batteries was beginning to run out, but in the hurry and confusion of our departure he had forgotten to bring any spares. It was therefore with difficulty that towards dawn, as the crack and boom of gunfire continued from the direction of Sewa City, we were able to make out the MRC Chairman himself announcing with regret that PRA rebels had entered the capital. He declared Martial Law and ordered everyone off the streets 'so as not to hinder the operations of the security forces.'

'I am allowing only half an hour,' he went on, sounding as stern as Jogolo on the war path. 'Anyone found in the streets after half an hour will be considered a PRA rebel and shot on sight. You have been warned.'

'After telling people that there was no cause for alarm,' Mams muttered, sucking her teeth disgustedly. For his part, Dad expressed deep relief that both of their parents had, as he put it, 'crossed over', saying he didn't know how he would have coped if they'd had other people to worry about as well. Then he suddenly stopped short, which made me realise that he had remembered Melvina though he dared not mention her.

As the sound of the radio grew fainter and more distorted, Dad again scolded himself for forgetting to bring the spare batteries.

'Let me go up and get them,' I offered quickly; not because I was feeling brave, but because I was very anxious to find out what had happened to the Noahs whose house stood directly in the path of anyone emerging from the forest reserve. Mams protested at first but realising that a radio was essential at such a time, finally agreed to let me go.

Having picked up Dad's spare batteries, I went next door to carry out my plan. By this time, the surviving dogs had fallen asleep, exhausted after the eventful and terrifying night. I could see Gramma Cobola's 'Whisky' curled up under her orange tree. Since her gate had no padlock, I released the catch and tiptoed into the yard. Whisky stirred, raised his head, recognised my familiar smell and curled up tighter. I crept up the back stairs and knocked softly on the door.

'It's Manny, Gramma,' I said as loudly as I dared when I heard footsteps approaching. 'Manny…'

It was Modu who pulled back the bolts, but Gramma Cobola was right behind him, smelling as usual of the camphor balls in which she stored her clothing. The effect was somehow soothing after the extreme tension of the night.

'Boy, what are you doing here?' she demanded softly. 'Didn't you hear what the Chairman said?'

'Gramma, our radio is almost dead,' I explained.

She immediately understood why I had taken the risk of leaving our house and whispered, 'Come inside, my child, come inside,' before limping as fast as her unstable legs could take her, to fetch the batteries. On her return, she hustled me out of the door and told me to pay her later even before I asked for credit.

I now undertook a trip to the top of the hill, darting in and out of bushes along the way like an animal on the look out for hunters. I paused to survey the whole area before approaching the Noahs' house. Only Khalid was visible, leaning on the veranda railing, bare-chested in spite of the sharp Harmattan breeze. As I emerged, I saw him straighten up in alarm then exhale with relief when he realised who was approaching.

'*Copain*…it's you,' he said.

'How goes?' I asked

'Some of the bastards passed right by our house, but they just made a lot of noise with their stupid song, damned us all and went on their way.'

'Same thing happened down at our end,' I said. 'Where is everybody else?'

'Asleep, I think. Mama Abi gave us another scare when we heard them coming. We thought she was going to collapse again the way she was holding her head... '

Having sympathized with him over this added cause for anxiety I asked him to tell Hamida I had been to see them, adding on impulse, 'And tell her I love her with all my heart.'

Khalid sucked his teeth and rolled his eyes, pretending to be thoroughly fed up with my passion for his sister, but he promised to pass on the message which left me feeling as happy as one could be in the circumstances. I hurried back home to face my parents' anxious wrath.

<><><><><>

Dad growled, 'Where the hell have you been?' and when I said that, not knowing what might happen in the next few days, I had gone to pick up more batteries on credit, Mams scoffed, 'Do you really expect us to believe that going to Gramma Cobola took you twenty minutes?'

I was saved from having to confess my recklessness by another announcement on the radio. It was the Brigadier-General this time, telling us that he was easing the house arrest the MRC Chairman had imposed a few hours earlier. Until three p.m. people could move short distances out of their compounds if they felt safe enough to do so.

We returned upstairs soon afterwards, but for the rest of the day spoke in hushed voices and never strayed far from the radio. Since we lived well outside Sewa City, we had hardly any idea of what was actually going on there, but realised the situation was extremely dangerous because of the continual pounding and cracking of artillery fire, the faint smell of explosives in the air, and the broad trails of grey smoke streaking the hazy sky in the distance. A few minutes after five p.m. *Focus on Africa* came on the BBC. The entire programme was devoted to reports and analyses of the terrible events taking place in the country.

As we listened to the reporter's agitated account, we stared at each other, crying out in horror from time to time or clapping our hands to our mouths. The PRA had burst into State House and other government offices. Some senior members of the MRC had been shot dead. Others had fled. The PRA had stormed the prison gates and released all its inmates, including hardened criminals who then joined the mayhem. The PRA were setting public buildings on fire. The Town Hall and the Ministry of Finance had gone up in flames.

A later edition of the programme provided even more horrifying details of the calamity that had befallen Sewa City. The PRA were spraying entire streets with kero and setting private houses on fire. The reporter said he could see dead bodies on the ground. The main telephone exchange, post office and central police station were now ablaze. The PRA had captured the main power station plunging the entire city into darkness, the only light, the red-orange glow of burning buildings. When he said they were receiving reports that a mosque was on fire with more than one hundred people trapped inside, shaking her head in bemusement, Mams cried out, 'What kind of people are these?' echoing my own thoughts and, no doubt, Dad's as well. 'If their quarrel is with the MRC, why are they creating such havoc for everybody else, and against the country itself? I can't understand it…I can't understand it.'

'It must be drugs,' Dad said. 'People have been saying that they take drugs. It has to be drugs. Who in their right minds would do such terrible and senseless things?'

In the end, the catalogue of destruction and carnage became too much for them to bear. They cried out each other's names almost at the same moment, '*Millie*!' '*Ola*!' then, their long estrangement forgotten in the intensity of their anguish, they reached out to clutch each other and sobbed as if their hearts were breaking.

Inspite of the horrible situation, there was a bit of joy mingled with my own distress as I left them.

<><><><><>

Gradually, the security forces began to control the chaos in Sewa City. For several days after the attack, jet bombers, flown by the foreign troops, screamed over our heads on their way to drop their lethal cargo on suspected PRA hideouts. The security forces on foot also flushed PRA fighters from the most ingenious hiding places - among them, storm drains, the foundations of bridges and family vaults in all of the city's cemeteries. In their desire to exact revenge on the invaders, people living in the city were only too willing to assist the soldiers by whispering information which led to these arrests. And they committed atrocities of their own. I later heard that one group of enraged citizens managed to capture a rebel commander - one known as Colonel Odinga - whom they discovered in a slime-filled culvert near the Town Hall. He shot a few people, but the rest bravely pounced on him and beat him almost senseless before dousing a lorry tyre with petrol, forcing it over his head and setting it alight.

Meanwhile, many buildings in the city continued to smoulder and burn, and seeing that constant cloud of smoke deepened our fear. Except for occasionally sneaking outside to look for additional food or to check on our neighbours, we remained indoors all the time, even outside the curfew hours of 3 p.m. to 6 a.m.

Mams had two sacks of flour left. Every day, until it ran out, we baked bread which we shared with Gramma Cobola, Modu and other neighbours. We ate the bread and handfuls of boiled rice with sardines or corned beef or luncheon meat provided by Gramma Cobola. When the tinned food ran out, we ate rice and soaked '*garri*' with a trickle of palm-oil flavoured with crumbs of *Maggi* stock cubes.

About ten days passed in this fashion by which time, according to the news bulletins, the security forces had regained control of the city and were now carrying out 'mopping up' operations. That was when the retreating PRA fighters embarked on another 'Operation no mercy' - random hit and run raids more terrifying in their effect than the more organized invasion. BBC journalists reported seeing dozens of people with fresh amputations, as well as heaps of civilian corpses outside the city mortuary. They mentioned the vultures continuously circling over the building and swooping down from time to time to gorge themselves on carrion. We listened to the reports, shuddering.

<><><><>

George Town did not escape 'Operation no mercy'. About five-thirty p.m. on the fourteenth day, a large group of PRA desperadoes invaded our village. One of them, a boy who seemed younger than me, blasted his way into our house by the back door before we had time to take any steps to protect ourselves. In those moments of blind panic, my eyes registered only a dirty white bandanna, wild, bloodshot eyes and a raised scar that stretched diagonally across his forehead like a slender worm.

'Money, money; where is the money? Where is the money?' he yelled, gesturing menacingly with his AK-47.

Dad tried to maintain a dignified calmness, but I could see his hands shaking as he fumbled in his pockets and pulled out a few crumpled bank notes.

'This is all that we have in the house,' he said.

The meagre pickings drove the boy really wild. 'You are telling lies!' he shouted and, ignoring our screams, promptly riddled Dad with bullets. Mams must have guessed what would happen next for as Dad crumpled to the floor, she cried out, 'Run Manny, run...run!'

Before I could react, yelling more abuse at her, the boy swung his rifle round and gunned her down as coldly as he had shot Dad. As Mams collapsed to the floor, I wheeled round and dashed to the front of the house like an automaton, expecting bullets to slam into my back at any moment. But though the young man hurled more abuse at me, he did not fire his rifle again.

I leapt over the veranda railing, landing heavily on the small granite stones carpeting the ground in front of our house to warn us of approaching visitors. The impact of the fall tore my skin and twisted my left ankle under me. It was agony. I was moaning deep in my throat as I dragged myself to the back of the house and into the store. That was when the reality of what had happened hit me like a hammer blow and my teeth began to chatter in time with the shudders which took over my body. Within minutes a strong smell of burning seeped into the cellar, informing me that, like so many others in the city, my home was going up in flames.

As soon as I dared, I crept out of my hiding-place and tried to re-enter the house. Several times I tried, but the ferocity of the flames kept driving me back for this was February, it had not rained for months and the country was still in the grip of the Harmattan. The dry old timbers that formed the main walls and beams of my grandfather's house offered no resistance to the flames. The fire burned as far as the concrete floor, consuming everything in its path. In anguish too deep to be expressed then or described now, I sat on the ground watching the destruction of my world, and seriously wishing that the rebel boy had gunned me down too.

I still ask myself why he let me go. Perhaps he had intended to force me at gunpoint to join the PRA, decided it wasn't worth the trouble to chase me when I fled, and turned his attention to looting our house before setting it on fire. Who knows? Who can fathom the thought processes of a mind as unhinged by drugs as his must have been?

I might have been safe enough from the flames in the concrete store, but didn't dare to chance it. Once I'd given up trying to enter the house, I sought refuge in the bread oven and curled up in cold ashes, grateful now that I had still not grown much taller than Dad. That thought made me remember that Mams and Dad had ceased to exist and I would have nothing but their charred remains to bury.

Ah! This is still too hard. I have to stop for a while.

<><><><><>

They departed as swiftly as they had come - those murderers - leaving behind scenes from the worst of nightmares - tongues of orange flames hazy through billowing smoke; crashing timbers and exploding glass; bodies lying in the road, other human forms dashing here and there in utter confusion, or standing as immobile as stone pillars; cries and curses hurled at the black sky where stars dared to twinkle as if this were an ordinary night.

By dawn the fires had died down for want of anything else to devour. Acrid smoke and smouldering embers lingered in the ruins, and an eerie silence reigned like the aftermath of a terrific storm. A sudden gust of Harmattan breeze cut through my clothing, making me shiver again as I emerged from the bread oven, painfully got to my feet and limped towards the back steps. Only then did I notice that Gramma Cobola's house seemed to have escaped the fires except for a coating of soot. I was contemplating this miracle in a daze when, like a bow-legged ghost, Mr. Togbah appeared from the mist and smoke. The sight of what had once been our house, and of me standing there like a zombie, must have told him all he needed to know because, having greeted me with a subdued, 'My young friend,' he asked no questions, only climbed the back steps and walked onto the concrete floor which, with the store and bar below it, was all that remained of No. 4 Macaulay Street. Presently, Gramma Cobola and Modu also appeared, both equally lost for words.

Gramma Cobola wrapped my parent's charred remains in a white tablecloth she had embroidered herself and prayed over the shallow grave Mr. Togbah dug behind the bathroom and toilet. Then she pulled off her head tie, telling me to bind up my foot which, by this time, was so swollen that it looked like one of Mr.Togbah's loaves.

'God will punish those bastards, Manny,' she muttered with venom in her voice. 'He will surely punish them.'

Still numb from the shock of it all, I had no thoughts or wishes about anything, so instead of responding to what Gramma Cobola said, I told her that I was going up the hill to see what had happened to the Noahs.

'With that foot?' she exclaimed, concern etching fresh creases on her forehead. 'You will make it worse-oh.' But ignoring her warning, I strapped up the ankle and began the agonising climb towards the Noahs' house, leaning on Mr. Togbah's sturdy arm.

As we ascended the hill, we saw that a similar pattern of destruction was repeated all along the way. This house destroyed, that one mysteriously intact. Half-way up, we encountered Mr. Danso sitting outside the ruins of their family home looking completely crazy - stark naked, his hair knotty as if it had never been touched by a comb. He didn't even raise his head when we passed; just continued mumbling to himself and jerking about as if insects were attacking him. My heart began to pound as we neared the top of the hill and a feeling of dread settled at the pit of my stomach with the weight of a grinding stone.

The Anglican vicarage seemed intact but St. Stephen's church and its primary school where Mams had been a teacher for so many years, were both blackened ruins open to the sky. So was the Noah's house.

There were quite a few people in the compound - the walking wounded, so to say. Some of them were talking in hushed voices while others stood in silence, one hand supporting a cheek or both arms flung over their heads in utter distress. When there was no immediate sign of any of the Noahs, my courage failed for a moment, slowing my footsteps even further. Then I caught sight of Pa Noah. He was sitting on the grass, legs outstretched with a blood-soaked pad over one eye. He seemed to be narrating something. As we drew nearer, I heard him describing in a feeble, hesitant voice, how Mama Abi, who lay motionless beside him, had suffered a stroke after being raped in front of her family. She was alive, but paralysed down one side and speechless. My '*copain*', Khalid, was lying on his back by his parents, blood caked on his face, shot dead while trying to prevent Hamida's abduction. *She* had subsequently been dragged into the forest.

The rest of that day remains a blur, thank God.

Chapter Fifteen

IN THE WAKE OF THE STORM

22-26 May 1997 (what happened between 14 March – 3 May)

God sends us angels when we need them. I strongly believe that now - human agents, though we don't always recognise them as such at the time. In the immediate aftermath of my personal tragedy, Mr. Togbah was mine. He stayed with me for the rest of that day and night and well into the next morning, quietly dropping words of comfort and encouragement in my ear as he helped me prepare for the journey into Sewa City to seek treatment for my injuries. With her permission, he made me crutches from Gramma Cobola's fence posts and filled a plastic bottle with water from the stream. He put it in the plastic bag containing my diaries, some cabin bread biscuits and bank notes Dad had hidden there, and hung the whole lot from my neck; then we started out. He could only go part of the way with me, he apologised, explaining that 'his lady' would be almost out of her mind with worry. After asking anxiously whether I could manage on my own, he promised to look me up in the hospital the very next day.

The debris left by destruction and panic littered the streets - heaps of rubble and charred timber, shards of broken glass, empty cartridges, motor car tyres and an amazing assortment of abandoned footwear. Avoiding these obstacles in my condition was a test of endurance, especially in the scorching heat which had rapidly despatched the morning chill. Within half an hour of my setting out, sweat was oozing out of every pore in my body and flowing into all its crevices. I was glad that I had thought of tearing strips from Gramma Cobola's head tie and wrapping them around my hands to protect them, otherwise they would surely have been rubbed raw by my damp crutches.

The only time I had ever seen so many people heading in the same direction was when going to and from football matches between 'Invincible Lions' and 'Sakoma Stars'. All sorts and generations of people filled the streets, from old men and women sprawling in pushcarts and wheelbarrows or clinging to the backs of younger men, their bony knees sticking out at angles, to lonely little children, bleating like lost sheep. Many people appeared as dirty and unkempt as I must have looked myself with my ash-covered clothes, sweaty body and knotty hair. At frequent intervals I had to join noisy, restless queues waiting to pass through makeshift checkpoints where soldiers did rough body searches before allowing us to continue on our way. Finally they began to warn us that curfew would start shortly which meant that we had to secure shelter for the rest of that day and night and to do it fast.

With so many other people seeking refuge, it proved difficult to find suitable accommodation. In the end I settled for a roofless house with only gaping squares where the windows had been. At least thirty other people were already inside, sitting side by side on the blackened concrete floor in what must once have been the parlour. They were leaning against walls also black with soot. As I hopped into the room, they turned as one to regard me with hollow, lightless eyes. A few of them responded to my greeting without interest then, as I imagined exhausted survivors of a shipwreck would behave, returned to staring silently into space, their hands lying on their laps like abandoned objects. Without my asking, they made room for me on the floor where I crumpled like a half empty sack. By this time, my injured lower leg felt as if strong fingers were pinching it non-stop in a dozen places. In my agony, it seemed that evening would never come, let alone the night; but at length the room darkened and the first mosquitoes whined in my ear.

<><><><><>

Among the stream of vehicles that passed as I struggled along the road early the next morning, was a military jeep, its driver steadily pressing the horn. It swerved past me then screeched to a halt, reversed and to my greatest surprise and not a little apprehension, pulled up beside me. Out jumped an officer - obviously foreign, eyebrows and moustache jutting out like bamboo roofs, a huge patch of sweat across his shirt. My heart jumped when I noticed his pistol pointing straight at me.

'Where are you from?' he barked.

'Ge-George Town, Sir,' I replied, trembling as I pointed one of my crutches in the direction from which I had come. I briefly narrated what had taken place there and told him I was on my way to the hospital.

'And how did you manage to escape?' he demanded. 'Young men like you do not usually escape from those thugs. They are either killed or else taken by force to become rebel fighters.'

His voice had a hard, suspicious edge to it and beneath those menacing brows, his eyes bored into me like a drill. I thought my suffering and helplessness must be obvious to everyone, but only after running his hands all over my body, did he offer me a lift.

'We cannot afford to take any chances,' he said when he was satisfied. 'Those guys are clever , you know - up to all kinds of tricks. They pretend to be beggars, to be crippled, to be simpletons, even to be crazy...'

As the driver ploughed his way through the teeming streets, the officer kept up a running commentary, pointing out various battlegrounds in the fight to save the capital. Like a stranger in a foreign country, my eyes roamed from one sight to another - vultures still circling expectantly overhead; bullet-pitted walls; charred skeletons of public buildings and people's homes; torn up streets; burnt-out vehicles. The destruction was even worse than I had imagined it from the BBC reports and such was my shock and horror that I don't think I could have uttered a single word even to save my life. Nor was I the only one so affected. The officer had stopped for three other sick-looking people - all women. They now occupied the back seat of the jeep with me and their gasps, cries and sobs punctuated his commentary from time to time. At length, he said, not unkindly,

'My people, war is a very nasty business-oh. Everybody loses; even the ones who gain the so-called victory. But we human beings never learn. That's why there will always be work for people like me.'

Eventually, we arrived at Queen Victoria Hospital where such an agitated sea of humanity surged at its huge iron gates that I was relieved when, as I made to descend with the other passengers, the officer told me to stay where I was.

'For the time being, this hospital only treats medical cases,' he informed me. '*You* are going to one of the places where they treat injuries like yours. Foreign doctors work there - Doctors without Borders - that is what they call themselves. They go all over the world - wherever there are poor people who need help.'

After another half an hour or so, we left scenes of recent battles behind and everything appeared almost normal, until we approached the bridge which linked the eastern side of the city to its western suburbs. Here, the officer remarked with savage pleasure,

'This is where we really dealt with those dirty dogs. Their bodies were piled over there and under the bridge like old mattresses - more than one hundred of them.'

I peered out of the jeep with a shudder, but little evidence of that life and death struggle remained except for the bullet holes that scarred the surrounding buildings.

It wasn't long afterwards that we turned off the main road and pulled up outside the wire mesh fence protecting a sprawling white building with an extensive compound. The side of the building bore a huge sign announcing that we had arrived at 'Dr. Konjo's Clinic'.

A number of people were going in and out of the gates and moving around or sitting in the compound, but nothing like the dense crowd besieging the main hospital. That officer must have taken a liking to me for some reason, because he escorted me inside and handed me over to a male nurse who soon had me out of my filthy clothes and into a strange garment that opened down the back exposing my bare buttocks. By that time I was too far gone to feel embarrassed.

'Don't worry about your money and exercise books,' the nurse responded kindly to my feeble inquiry. 'You will get them back later. They are perfectly safe. Tell me your name so I can start a record for you.'

Apparently I lost consciousness after that because some hours later, I found myself lying on a latex foam mattress on the green concrete floor, my left arm attached to a drip on a stand beside me. The room was excessively warm and smelled strongly of carbolic. I was briefly aware of several other mattresses on the ground, groans, whimpers and a general restlessness around me, before drifting off again. The next time I opened my eyes, someone was stroking my cheek and an ivory coloured face was looking down at me with a frown of concern. It belonged to a young woman with greyish semi-circles of skin below her exhausted brown eyes. Silky brown hair streaked her forehead in short sweat-soaked strands. Her frown almost vanished when she smiled.

'Ah, bon,' she said in French, then went on in English, 'You are back with us, Emmanuel. How are you feeling?'

I was still in agony and tried to tell her so through dry, cracked lips.

'You damaged your ankle badly,' she told me. 'A tendon has been torn and you cracked a bone. We have done some repairs and you will be on your feet again before too long…perhaps with a little limp, but, don't worry… not enough to put the girls off…'

She must have expected a smile at her little joke and when it failed to appear, simply said,'Okay. Go back to sleep now.'

That should have been the beginning of the end of my physical ordeal at least, but it wasn't, as I later discovered. My wound had become infected because it had been neglected for so many hours, and I was soon in the grip of a severe malaria attack as well. The nurses told me that I ran alarming temperatures which took many days to respond to antibiotics and chloroquine and made me thrash about on my mattress talking utter rubbish. However, four weeks later, Dr. Gerardeau, the ivory-skinned surgeon, gently twisted my ankle up and down and from side to side after glancing at my chart.

'Good,' she said. 'I'm very pleased, Emmanuel. Next week you will start getting up.'

She must have noticed anxiety etched on my face as I thanked her, because she went on to ask whether there was something else troubling me. I assured her that all was well, but it wasn't true. From time to time feelings of unbearable loneliness swept over me as I lay there remembering that all the people I loved and depended upon in one way or another had left me. I ached to hear my parents' voices, to feel Hamida's soft fingers clinging to mine and to exchange banter and jokes with Khalid. Getting back on my feet would mean having to face life alone and penniless at a time when most people in the country were suffering in one way or another. How and where would I live? I asked myself. Who would pay my fees? I would probably have to leave school without sitting my 'A' levels. There was Uncle Eku but he was thousands of miles away and I didn't even know how to contact him.

But I had reckoned without the humane services and resources of the International Red Cross. No sooner could I hobble about again with my new metal crutch, than Dr. Gerardeau sent me to their office in the hospital compound where I was greeted by the young man on duty. He asked my name and when I answered, promptly turned to a computer on his desk. I had seen these fascinating machines in films, but my only experience of them had been at the British Council library where the assistants used them to record loans and returns of books by shining a special light on small labels with mysterious uneven stripes. I had yet to experience the other marvels of which they were capable.

The young man's fingers skipped along the keyboard as he typed my name then, having pressed another key, he peered at the small screen in front of him, got to his feet and went to a safe standing in a corner. He returned with the information that he had some money for me which I could collect when I was discharged, before going to a metal cupboard from which he withdrew the plastic bag containing my diaries and my precious photograph of Hamida. To say I was amazed would be putting it mildly; and there were even greater marvels in store when he sat down and returned to peering at the screen.

'Are your parents' names Ola and Millicent Martin?' he enquired.

'Yes, but they are no more, 'I answered, feeling my throat tighten. 'The PRA killed them when they attacked George Town.'

He muttered condolences without moving his eyes from the screen which made me think him a cold, insensitive person. That is, until I realised that he must have heard similar answers so many times in recent weeks that he had probably lost some of his ability to express sympathy. I was about to ask him how he had obtained all this information, when he made my heart leap by saying, 'We have a contact for you in America.'

'What!' I exclaimed. 'You mean Mr. Eku Martin?'

'Exactly,' the young man replied. 'You are lucky.'

He looked so pleased to be able to give me good news that I

completely forgave him his earlier failure to comfort me over my bereavement. Later he told me that, frantic with worry, Uncle Eku had contacted the International Red Cross at their headquarters in Switzerland and the information he was able to provide had been passed on to the local office. More wonders were revealed when the young man linked me to Uncle Eku by satellite phone remarking, as he handed me the receiver, ' Wonderful, eh? You have to admire these white people for their technology.'

My first telephone conversation with Uncle Eku was so painful that I don't know how I managed it. At one point he interrupted my account of the tragedy to exclaim, 'Manny, I just can't believe it. I *can't* believe it. Ours is the last country in the *world* where I would have believed such things could happen - burning innocent people's houses? - raping old women? - chopping off people's hands and feet - even children - in this day and age? What has happened to that place in my absence?'

His voice was hoarse, as if he had been crying for days and was still close to tears, which made it difficult for me to control my own trembling lips. Eventually I heard him sigh; then he said, 'Anyway, let's get down to practical matters.'

I expected an invitation to live with him in America, but as Mams once told me, life is not a fairy tale.

'I want to sponsor you to come over here, Manny,' he went on, 'but right now, I can't afford it, and in any case, these things take time. But you're old enough to look after yourself now, aren't you?'

I had to agree.

'What I shall do is send you some money at once via the Red Cross, so you can rent a place to stay, replace some of your things, pay school fees and so on. I shall also try to send you some dollars by Western Union every month for your food and rent, etc. etc, okay? Call me collect at this number as soon as you are settled.'

Despite my sharp disappointment that I would not be escaping my painful memories and the miseries of my war-torn country any time soon, I was so touched by Uncle Eku's generosity and kindness that I once again had to struggle with tears.

'Manny, we are Africans,' he replied when I tried to thank him. 'My brother's child is my own. No way could I leave you to fend for yourself now that those dear people are gone. If you have any problems - any problems at all, just call me collect and I'll do what I can to help. Don't you ever think that you are alone, you hear me? God bless… and keep in touch, eh.'

That conversation made me remember Melvina again. Mr. Togbah had promised to look her up when he finally traced me to Dr. Konjo's Clinic; but he came back a few days later to report that her grandmother's house was among several burned to the ground along that street. He hadn't been able to find anyone in the area who could tell him what had become of the people who used to live there. For now, I can only trust that Melvina and her grandmother are safe somewhere. But I wonder if I shall ever see her again. Perhaps her mother will somehow get to know that Ola Martin's son is alive and get in touch with me one of these days - or perhaps Melvina herself will come looking for me when she's older. I really hope so.

<><><><>

I spent the next two weeks in a kind of limbo - not well enough to be completely discharged, but not ill enough to continue taking up space in the wards that was needed for serious cases. I moved to one of the green plastic tents in the small, makeshift camp for displaced persons and convalescents which the Red Cross had set up in the hospital's vast compound. This was where I experienced at first hand the sheer boredom of a refugee's life. Every day, after taking my turn at one of the two available standpipes outside to collect water for bathing, my sole occupation, since I had been advised to stay off my feet, was to sit around waiting for food or second-hand clothing to be distributed, or else hoping for a visitor. I had tried bringing my diary up to date, but the pen always remained motionless in my hand, somehow too heavy for me to move it across the page. Mr. Togbah's visits remained rare pleasures due to the distance between his camp and mine, and so the highlight of most days was the arrival of the pastors and aid workers who came to talk to us quietly about the need to forgive the PRA and the soldiers who had betrayed the country in such a disgraceful way. One of these people was a thin, young pastor wearing black-rimmed spectacles which tended to drop to the end of his nose. He was known as Brother Bob and came to Dr. Konjo's Clinic twice a week, usually in the afternoon, looking tired and sweaty yet completely at peace as if he had worked successfully through the list of goals he had set himself that day.

The first time Brother Bob spoke to me about forgiving the rebels, I laughed in his face - rudely.

'Forgive those animals, sir!' I said. 'That is not possible. Not after what they did to us.'

I then launched into an emotional account of all the injuries I had suffered at the hands of the PRA. Brother Bob listened patiently, nodding now and then, not once interrupting the torrent of words.

'Small brother, I know, I know,' he said, when I finally fell silent. 'The suffering has been terrible, but you have to forgive them…Are you a Christian, by the way?'

'Yes, sir. A Catholic.'

He paused before going on as if, like Solade, he also thought Catholics rather dubious Christians.

'Anyway,' he said, 'I hope you know what the Bible says about forgiveness.'

Before I could answer, he quoted chapter and verse, no doubt hoping that the authority of scripture would melt my stony heart. However, though I was well acquainted with those particular texts, reminding me of them did nothing to soften my heart. The rage I had felt as I ran for my life had subsided in the aftermath of the attack on George Town - quenched by the trauma of losing my parents, my home, my best friend and my sweetheart in one deadly blow. Besides, it had all happened incredibly fast; and then I had fallen ill. Anger returned on my first afternoon outside the ward when I saw two small girls playing. Each of them had lost a hand to PRA cutlasses so they could only maintain the rhythm of the game they were playing by stamping their feet. In spite of this disability, they were thoroughly enjoying themselves, collapsing in fits of merry laughter every time they caught each other out. It was a sight to hearten anybody watching them; but it did not have that effect on Emmanuel. My own gaze became fixed on those ugly stumps at the ends of their arms which could never clap again or pick up children.

'Why? Why?' I raged aloud.

Several people gave me curious looks, but no one attempted to provide an answer. The stronger I became, the fiercer my anger burned, until I finally screamed at Brother Bob one afternoon, 'I don't want to hear about forgiveness any more. They are not human beings.'

Without another word, he got to his feet, pressed my shoulder and moved on.

<><><><><>

Immediately after he left me, I heard my name.

'You, Emmanuel, come here.'

The voice belonged to Mrs. Binda, the tough-talking, no-nonsense woman in charge of food at the camp, thus providing my two meagre meals a day. As I approached, she eyed me up and down with strong disapproval.

'You see that young man,' she said, 'the one you shouted at just now… Let me tell you something. There is nothing you have suffered that he has not suffered too. Nothing. As a matter of fact, he has suffered more than many people. He lost every member of his close family up-country, and then his young wife and baby and everything he had in this world. You should listen to him instead of behaving like an unbrought-up so and so.'

Knowing what my own parents thought of bad manners in general, and especially bad manners towards my elders, I was already feeling ashamed of myself. Mrs. Binda's information deepened my remorse and I apologised meekly.

'Don't beg my pardon,' she flung at me over her shoulder as she flounced off to oversee the preparation of our main meal of the day. 'Beg his.'

Which is what I did the very next time Brother Bob appeared; whereupon he promptly put his arm around my shoulder, and pulled me aside.

'Small brother,' he said. 'It's not easy, I know - I've been through it. But the Master commands us to forgive, and who am I to refuse? If you are a Christian, He should be your Master too.... Let me tell you something. Whenever I remembered what the rebels did and I felt anger rising, I used to say, 'Master, thy will be done. I forgive them.' At first even thinking those words, was harder than...than drinking quinine, especially when I heard that some of the rebels were going around boasting about their exploits. It might have been easier if I had heard that they were showing signs of being sorry for what they had done. But...I just kept on repeating those words, repeating those words, repeating those words. And you know, maybe it was coincidence, but unexpected blessings started coming my way. First of all, one of my church members offered me a room, so I was able to move out of this place - my wife and baby girl died here, you know. Then somebody else gave me a safari suit and I got a brand new Bible...O, so many blessings. Small brother, obedience is worth it. Believe me!'

This time I hung my head respectfully, but remained silent, thinking that the damage that boy had done was too recent, too fresh. I felt entitled to hold on to my rage, almost as a mark of respect to my parents.

On another day, Brother Bob told me how he had been guided to visit one of the camps where young PRA fighters - those who managed to run away or had been captured - were being helped to return to normal life.

'That was the most wonderful blessing of all, small brother. When I met those PRA boys face to face and heard their stories...' His hand made a sweeping motion across his chest. 'Compassion filled my heart to overflowing. I had no more difficulty with forgiveness after that.'

Unimpressed, it was in a sullen tone that I muttered, 'How could you feel sorry for those...those animals?'

'When you meet them, you will understand how it was possible,' he answered serenely. 'And do you know what else forgiving them did for me? Since I lost my family, I had only been going through the motions of living - you know, getting up in the morning, doing this, doing that, then going to bed to lie awake for half the night. After that day, I slept like a baby. Small brother, decide to forgive them. I tell you, it's in your own interest... You know what, when the doctors give you the all clear, come to the camp with me.'

But I was still unwilling to release my sense of outrage and refused the invitation with a vigorous shake of my head. If he felt disappointed, Brother Bob hid it well.

'All right. When you are ready just let me know,' he said. If it happens after you are discharged, you can always find me at the back office of the Church of the Master on Jabez Ajayi St. I am there every day till about twelve o'clock.'

There he let the matter rest and changed the subject.

'Have you ever heard about the New Afrikan Movement?' he asked, taking me completely by surprise.

'You mean Mr. Azigidah?' I asked eagerly. 'So you were there that night!'

'O, yes. Nothing would have kept me away from a meeting like that. I wanted to hear what Mr Azigidah had to say because I had been asking myself why Africa is in such a mess. I refuse to believe that it is because we Africans are just incapable of managing our affairs…'

'And did you agree with his conclusion?' I asked.

'That we should all return to the old customs? No, I did not, but nor did I agree with those people who walked out. I believe in dialogue - in debating differences of opinion in a friendly way.'

'Even when it's something that goes against your religion?' I asked.

'Even then,' said Brother Bob. 'You don't have to compromise your principles. Small brother, debate and discussion sharpen the mind and help to prevent fighting…'

'I agree, sir, but when it comes to religion, even people who normally like to debate ideas - like one of my good friends who walked out - even people like him draw the line when it comes to ideas that challenge things in the Bible. He believes many of our traditional beliefs are demonic. In fact, I'm surprised that *you* didn't walk out too…'

'But that is exactly why I didn't walk out, small brother,' Brother Bob told me. 'That kind of gesture is for people who are afraid of being contaminated. The Master would not have done that because he *knew* he could not be contaminated. Knowing that God is always at their side, His followers should have that confidence too…'

Brother Bob's down-to-earth way of talking about religion so delighted me that I exclaimed,

'I wish I had known you long before this. You put these things in such a practical way…'

'That is because for me faith is a practical matter,' he laughed. 'If you are not seriously trying to live the teachings, don't call yourself a believer…Which brings me back to Africa. I agree with Brother Azigidah about one thing…that we are lacking in some sort of power. Where I differ is in the reason for that. *I* believe it's because too many Africans, and I do not exclude myself entirely, are afraid of too many things - afraid of evil spirits, afraid of each other, afraid of losing anything we have managed to acquire, afraid of sharing, afraid of being considered outsiders, afraid of having a bad name…' He lowered his voice to add, 'Small brother, many Africans are even afraid of God…'

'But Brother Bob…we're supposed to fear God,' I protested, shocked that *he,* of all people, would say such a thing. 'The Bible says that over and over again'.

'That is Old Testament religion,' he said in a tone that would allow no contradiction. '*My* Master had a higher understanding and according to Him, God is our father - were you afraid of your father? We are to have great reverence for God and worship Him, yes, but not to be afraid of Him as if He would otherwise harm us. We are to love Him like a father because that is the way *He* loves us. And we should act towards other people with the same family love because. all of us are God's children. When that happens, everything else follows - respect for each other's rights, concern for the underprivileged, honest dealings, a sense of justice, and so on. In my humble opinion, *that*, more than anything else is what will help Africa to start solving her problems. Do you think this terrible war would have happened and gone on for nearly five years if there had been more of that kind of love in this country?'

'Brother Bob, you should start your own movement,' I remarked, only joking, but he took me seriously.

He said, 'I've thought of that, you know, but I have too much on my plate already... Hurry up and get well, then you can help me set something up. I think you and I could work well together in spite of your hard attitude to those poor boys…'

My response was a sceptical 'Hmm.'

'I mean it,' he replied. 'I feel it in my heart.'

<><><><><>

I had a very strange dream that night, perhaps as a result of that conversation. I was standing on the edge of a precipice in a deserted place, when somebody called my name. The voice was whispery and attached to neither face nor form but before I could flee in terror, it added quickly, 'Don't be afraid. We are friends.'

I received an impression of a familiar presence, loving and calm, and began to feel less frightened though ten times more confused.

'First of all, we want to tell you that we are all right,' the voice continued. 'Very much all right. In fact, much better than we were on the other side… And we had a wonderful surprise when we crossed over... There is no more pain of any kind.'

Remembering all the broken, bleeding bodies I had recently seen, I thought I must be in heaven and the voice must, in some mysterious way, be the combined spirits of Dad and Mams.

'And we shall tell you another secret,' continued the ghostly voice. 'Time as we knew it before means nothing over here. The past, the present, the future - they are all part of one unbroken cycle.'

'But I don't understand,' I said. 'Have I crossed over too?'

I had a distinct impression of amusement as the voice answered, 'No, and you won't be doing so for a long time.'

'Then what is happening?' I asked.

'We have come to cheer you up, that's all. We are going to show you something.'

Before I had time to wonder what was coming next, I was

swooping down the precipice as if borne on the back of an enormous bird. In no time, we were flying over the familiar hills and valleys of my own country. My mouth fell open.

Wide, straight roads with not a pothole in sight criss-crossed the entire country. In the cities, of which there were at least six, some larger than others, the borders of all the streets were paved, so that people did not have to pay much attention to the traffic as they went about their business. In every city, rows and clusters of neat one-storeyed houses nestled among mango, pawpaw, palm and breadfruit trees, each within its own compound. Gone were all the makeshift shacks with their flimsy roofs held down with small rocks. Gone were the heaps of stinking garbage. Green parks adorned with trees and flowers of every hue, sparkling fountains and stone benches graced these cities, as well as sheltered, orderly markets and shopping arcades. Each city boasted a large white hospital and other public buildings in styles of architecture I had never seen before.

We continued our flight, diving low for closer inspection, soaring upwards to cover distances. I saw the chameleon-green of rice fields which covered vast stretches of land, and miles of plantain and banana groves and yam heaps and palm-trees standing in straight rows like troops on parade. They were laden with bunches of ripe, red palm-nuts ready for the harvest. Mango, orange and pineapple orchards, all neatly laid out, added to the impression of peaceful prosperity.

As we sailed over the capital, I caught my breath. All the small villages to the east had merged with the city to form a magnificent metropolis. From east to west a wide road followed the curves of the coastline so that vehicles not bound for the city itself travelled with the ocean to one side of them. As with the rest of the country, all the dirty shanty towns had been replaced by pleasant communities. Hillside mansions still stared haughtily down on the city, but since the mean shanties of the poor no longer existed, their opulence no longer offended the eyes.

'Ah', I sighed, gazing on the scene, my longing intense. 'If only…if only...'

Finally we hovered over the very centre of the capital city and I was able to study its inhabitants more closely. People seemed well fed, well dressed and glad to be alive. A steady hum of laughter and conversation floated towards me from the houses below, as did the beat and throb of music from passing vehicles. Strong-limbed children skipped and danced in sandaled feet, making up little songs to accompany their games. This was my country as it was meant to be.

'Are you telling me that we shall get from where we are now to this...this paradise?' I asked.

'We are saying it is possible,' replied the voice.

'But how?' I wanted to know.

'You who are left, can make it possible by using your brains and muscles,' it told me. 'That is all God has ever given to anyone in the world - brain and muscle. If you want your country to be like this, use your own - as well as your heart.'

I awoke on that word 'heart'. It echoed what Brother Bob had said the day before, making me feel that the coincidence must mean something.

Chapter Sixteen

PICKING UP THE PIECES

28 May 1997 (what happened between 5 May and 14 May)

A few days after that dream, Dr. Gerardeau examined my ankle again and said,'Well, Emmanuel, I think we can release you today, but please treat that ankle with respect for a while longer. Not too much standing on it yet...'

By this time, Uncle Eku had kept his promise and sent me 100 US dollars, so I thanked Dr. Gerardeau, collected my money from the Red Cross office and limped away from Dr. Konjo's Clinic to attempt to put the pieces of my life together again.

I returned to George Town like a homing pigeon, despite the tragic circumstances of my departure. The journey took much longer than I expected since it wasn't easy to travel from one end to the other of a city which had more than doubled its population in a matter of months. I had to change taxis three times, take a minibus for part of the way, then trek for the last bit of the journey. By the time I arrived at Macaulay Street junction, my ankle was throbbing painfully and I only had an hour to spare before the start of the curfew which remained in place though it had been extended to six in the evening. Almost immediately I recognised Modu's bony figure coming in my direction, carrying a bottle of kero.

Before I could call out to him, Modu recognised me, let out a joyful shout and came running. For several minutes we stood there repeating each other's names as if we had met by chance in a foreign country.

'What happened after I left?' I asked when we finally started up Macaulay Street.

'Many people left George Town that same day,' Modu told me. 'Red Cross people came with soldiers and took Pa Noah and his wife and some others away. Gramma's son came to look for her the next morning and took us to stay with him in town. We were there until people said the rebels had gone back up-country - about one month -

then Gramma said she wanted to come back to her own place. She and her son's wife…they don't see eye to eye.'

We had arrived at Gramma Cobola's gate and having caught sight of me through the spaces in the fence, Whisky was wagging his whole body, almost tying himself up in knots with delight.

Before following Modu into the yard, I went a little further up the road into our own yard and to the mound under which Mr. Togbah had buried Dad and Mams. Afterwards, feeling utterly sick at heart, I paused for a moment to look at the blackened ruins of my home. Modu was waiting for me at the gate and I asked him what happened to Pa Noah and Mama Abi.

'They live in town,' he answered. 'Behind Pa Noah's shop. Mama Abi is better, but she is still unable to walk or talk properly.'

That news depressed me further. A sigh escaped.

'And Hamida - any news?' I asked.

Modu's face clouded over, reflecting my own misery.

'No, nothing. But two city girls came back last week. They ran away.'

My heart leapt with a hope I hadn't realised was only dormant, not dead. I gripped Modu's shoulders, almost rattling the poor boy's bones in my eagerness to find out more.

'Do you know whether they have spoken about any other girls?'

Modu, however, had as usual picked up this news by eavesdropping on Gramma Cobola's conversations. He had nothing more to tell me.

<><><><>

'Boy! Is that you?' exclaimed Gramma Cobola herself a few minutes later, her flabby arms outstretched in welcome, her eyes raised in exultation. 'Praise God Almighty!'

She clasped me to the warm, soft cushion of her chest exuding camphor vapours as usual. 'And you are walking properly again. Thank you, Jesus! Ah, Manny...hmm. What happened? Tell me…'

She listened intently as I related the events of my life since leaving George Town to seek medical help. When I mentioned that I intended to sleep in our store that night and look for a place to rent in the neighbourhood, she told me off for even considering such a thing and invited me to stay with her. The room on offer had barely enough space for the narrow iron bed it contained and a rickety wooden chair; but I was grateful. Glad also to be able to put a little extra cash in the old woman's pockets and, at least for the time being, to spend much less on accommodation than I would otherwise have done.

I linked up with my other *copains* two weeks ago, after going to their houses with fear and trembling, not knowing what I would find. I was so glad to find them both safe and well and their homes intact. I don't think I could have borne it if I had lost them as well. They seemed even more relieved to see me than I to see them. Apparently two more of our school mates lost their lives during the rebel attack, and three St. Peter's boys were forced to join the PRA at gunpoint. The nightmare continues because there has been no news of them since their abduction.

15 June 1997

Schools reopened today. Strange atmosphere at St. Peter's, as if there was a shortage of oxygen or something, probably because everyone is still more or less traumatised. Also, many boys and staff were missing, including Mammy B. Apparently she and her family managed to escape to England. I was very glad to see Jogolo again though he looks ten years older. He represents the world I once knew, where nothing much happened and even though we didn't have much, we used to feel safe. Jogolo said prayers for the families of the dead and missing boys and staff, and there was another huge collective sigh. We have to repeat the school year because we are so far behind with the syllabus. Just as well. I am incapable of any serious studying.

Solade and Chico talked of nothing but the PRA attack during break. I didn't want to hear any of it, but it was comforting to be with them, so I stayed though I did not take part in the conversation. After a while they noticed my silence and kept quiet.

20 June 1997

I met Mr. Togbah on the way home from school. He has found work as a security man but says that if I start making bread again, he will come back to me. Glad on both counts. Perhaps I shall start again one day, but definitely not now. My energy level is still close to zero.

Went to see the Noahs this p.m. They greeted me warmly, but I felt very sad to be there - Pa Noah with one eye, Mama Abi sitting as silently as a bag of rice, no Khalid and no Hamida. I didn't stay long, but promised to visit them often.

I also went to see Father Bassey because arranging a proper funeral for Mams and Dad has been on my mind. Had to *beg* him to include Dad in a mass for Mams next week, which means I have to go to Confession, which means I will have to be a hypocrite. I don't see the point of confessing sins unless you are going to give them up and I can't forgive those rebels. In fact I want to kill all of them in the nastiest way possible, especially the one who murdered my parents and destroyed my life.

Hmm. So much to do between now and next week. Buying coffins will finish Uncle Eku's money. I must call him tomorrow.

25 June 1997

Buried Dad and Mams in George Town cemetery this a.m. Lovely sunshine throughout, but heavy rain later. Very quiet ceremony. Only Modu, Brother Bob, Mr. Togbah and *les copains* accompanied me to the cemetery. Gramma Cobola couldn't climb the hill.

I am so happy that Mams and Dad were at one again before they died. So sad that they had to die in that horrible way and that I shall never see them again; but I feel a bit better now that they have been buried properly.

5 July 1997

The curfew has been extended to midnight, so security must have improved a lot. I actually took pleasure in the sight of lush green mango trees against the clear blue sky while walking to school this morning. As they say, life goes on.

10 July 1997

At last! Today no one even mentioned February 27. It was almost like old times, except that Khalid was missing. 'Oh, my *copain*! Rest in perfect peace.

Chico says a national chapter of 'New Afrikans,' was formed last week and he has joined it. He invited us to the inauguration ceremony on Saturday which will include a special pouring of libation and a petition to our ancestors because, he says 'Africa is finished unless they intervene on our behalf.'

I have promised to attend but as expected, Solade declined, saying that communicating with the dead is spiritualism which the Bible forbids. It was a statement guaranteed to irritate Chico and he did not let it pass. He said, 'The Bible belongs to white people. That's what they used to brainwash Africans. Before our forefathers knew what was happening, those people had stolen our countries, organised them to suit themselves and then took our wealth to increase their own. Look at the Chinese and Japanese and Indians. They stuck to their own religions and traditions. That is why they are now competing with white people. *We* Africans have to commune with our ancestors more often or else we shall never prosper.'

Solade's usually easygoing attitude changed in a flash and he said rudely, 'What rubbish. You are only echoing that Mr Azigidah.'

At which point I decided to intervene before the argument became a full-blown quarrel again.

'Talking about Mr. Azigidah…,' I said hurriedly and began to tell them about my conversation with Brother Bob and the dream in which I saw our country so wonderfully transformed. They both agreed that the dream must be some sort of message, which started another argument - as to its source - God or other dubious spirits. I completely lost patience with them then and demanded to know why it mattered where the message came from? I said,

'What is important is whether or not it makes good sense and whether or not it is worth doing something about it.'

'Yes, it makes sense,' Solade admitted and for once Chico agreed with him. I felt a sudden surge of energy when Solade exclaimed, 'Hey, *copains*, why don't we start a different movement to promote those ideas? A movement for young people - forget about the old ones - *they* are past it. We'll say that nobody who is over thirty-five can join …'

'At least, not as a full member with voting rights,' I interjected, thinking of Brother Bob. 'We can have honorary members and we can invite older people whom we respect to give talks and lead debates and discussions.'

Chico looked much less enthusiastic than Solade, which made me suspect that he was afraid a movement like that might soon be taken over by the kind of not-African-enough people he objected to. I must have increased his wariness by suggesting that we call the movement 'Love is power,' because it was with a touch of ridicule that he said, 'And what will you call the members - Lovers?'

'Of course not,' I replied, crossly. 'Who would take us seriously? We can call the movement 'LIP' for short and just call ourselves members of LIP.'

'O… Okay. I'm interested,' he said. 'But that does not mean I won't continue supporting New Afrikans.'

'Did anyone ask you to?' Solade said.

Chico seemed to warm to the idea after that and even contributed to our discussion about the aims and objectives of LIP.

All in all, this has been one of my better days. Felt less like a zombie and my ankle hardly hurt me at all.

15 July 1997

Went to the city this morning to show Brother Bob the draft constitution we drew up for LIP last Saturday. It took me two whole hours to fight my way through the crowds in the street. In some places, I couldn't even see the ground and simply moved forward with the crowd as if we were coming from a football match. Will our capital city ever be the same again?

I hadn't seen Brother Bob since the funeral and it warmed my heart when he rose, almost shouting with pleasure at the sight of me. He was delighted with the LIP idea and *I* was delighted when he said, 'And it so happens that I won't be thirty-five till next July, so I am qualified to become a full member... You see! I told you we could work together. '

He skimmed through the draft constitution then pushed up his glasses which, as usual, had dropped to the end of his nose.

'Do you guys realise what these aims and objectives are saying, especially with the present situation in the country - *to promote love and unity among our people…?*

'I don't understand…,' I said.

'I am thinking about the PRA fighters,' Brother Bob continued. 'At least the ones who have laid down their arms and asked for forgiveness. Small brother, they are our people too, you know...'

'But they still have to be brought to justice,' I replied, sulky again.

'Yes, but what is justice in this situation?'

I had never seen Brother Bob look so grave. 'I'm not talking about their leader or the commanders and those treacherous so-called protectors of the state. *They* are grown men and should certainly answer for their crimes. I am talking about the boys and girls - *children*, small brother, children who were given drugs and forced to maim and kill people.'

'What about them?'

Instead of answering my question, Brother Bob again invited me to the camp, saying, 'Small brother, I strongly believe you will see things in a different light when you see some of those young people for yourself. *Then* we can discuss the whole thing again.' Reluctantly, very reluctantly, out of respect for his dedication and gratitude for his kindness, I have agreed to go with him at the end of the month, but secretly, I am hoping the weather will be so bad that he'll have to put off the visit.

Chapter Seventeen

FACE TO FACE WITH KILLERS

30 July 1997

There are some days which I have to record in full. Yesterday was one of them.

The weather did not oblige so I accompanied Brother Bob to a camp near one of the fishing villages. We had to take four minibuses because each one we joined was going a certain distance and no further. The last one stank of rotten fish. Each time we had to change transport, I said to myself: This man is an angel! - taking all this time and trouble to go and see those murderers. And using his own money.

The camp looks like some sort of military barracks, with six, long, low buildings in a compound surrounded by a link-mesh fence more than six feet high. Brother Bob called the buildings Nissen huts and told me they have been there since the colonial days. Strange looking things. Two muscular guys armed with rifles were guarding the gate. The one who let us in greeted Brother Bob with a grin that revealed filed incisors and the question, 'Pastor, what have you brought for us today?'

'My friend, you know all of us are in the same leaking canoe,' Brother Bob replied. 'In fact, you people are better off than me. Every day you get rations from *World Hope*. *I* have to twist and turn before I can eat.'

'A man of God like you?' The other guard said, looking incredulous. '*You* should not have to twist and turn for anything. Doesn't God provide for you?'

'Of course He does,' said Brother Bob. 'He shows me how to twist and turn.'

I joined in the laughter that reply caused, and it was on that jovial note that we proceeded to the admin building and knocked on the door.

So far there had been no sign of the inmates of the camp, but I could hear singing coming from one of the other buildings.

'This is a boys' camp.' Brother Bob explained as we waited to be let in. 'They sleep in those buildings over there.'

I tried to take an interest in these bits of information but somehow felt no curiosity whatsoever.

The camp manager is called Mr. Deed - an American. He has a deep slow voice like Sylvester Stallone - well built, with curly grey hair and blue eyes that twinkle. I liked him at once.

'You all go right ahead to Block C,' he said after Brother Bob had introduced me. 'They are having their daily fellowship at the moment. Emmanuel will meet the mentors and see how we work…Better go in by the back.'

As we entered the room, about forty heads turned in our direction and one of the four adults seated at the front called out, 'Brother Bob! You are welcome. Come in and join us with your friend.'

We sat on a bench along the wall near the mentors' chairs. The singing had already come to an end before we arrived and some kind of truth session was just beginning. One by one, boys were coming to the front to say how and why they became PRA fighters and what they had done. I didn't pay much attention to the speakers at first, preferring to scrutinise the audience.

As far as I could judge, the boys varied in age from about eight to sixteen. A few looked rather blank, as if they had lost their souls forever; but most of them were sitting alertly upright, hope and fear mingled in their expressions. I felt that they knew they deserved to be punished for their terrible deeds but all the same wanted desperately to be allowed to put the past behind them. I don't know what I expected, but seeing them now in their blue T-shirts and khaki shorts - cleaned up and reasonably well fed - I found it hard to believe that most of those boys had spent years committing murder and mayhem. They looked so ordinary. So very ordinary. I began to listen more attentively to the confessions and in doing so, started to understand why Brother Bob said they were victims themselves, badly damaged both by uncaring governments always playing politics, and by ruthless manipulators. As Brother Bob had predicted, my heart was beginning to soften slightly towards them when the next boy came forward to give his testimony.

He came from the back, which is probably why I hadn't noticed him before. As he reached the front of the room my eyes zeroed in on a raised scar stretched diagonally across his forehead. I knew at once that this was the boy who murdered my parents because it would have been too much of a coincidence for another boy of similar age to have an identical disfigurement. Time rolled rapidly back. It was early evening and I was in George Town again, facing a red-eyed boy screaming abuse and waving an AK-47. But there was one big difference. This time, *I* had the advantage of surprise. Without thinking, I leapt to my feet, shouting, 'He is the one! He is the one! ' and, as hot blood rushed to my head, sprang at him. Total pandemonium. We crashed to the ground, my fingers digging into his neck. I had begun to choke the life out of him before anybody tried to stop me.

'*You* killed my mother, you bastard,' I panted, squeezing harder as he thrashed about desperately trying to free himself. '*You* killed my father.'

'Small brother, STOP IT! STOP IT!'

Brother Bob's desperate appeal seemed to come from a long way off, though he was yelling in my ear. In his determination to save me from becoming a killer myself, he started prising my fingers away from the boy's throat, not caring how much he hurt me in the process. When he finally succeeded, he too was breathing hard. I remained in a crouching position, my eyes burning with frustration and hatred.

'*He* is the one that killed my mother and father,' I said through clenched teeth, my chest still heaving. 'And he burned down our house…'

'Yes, Emmanuel,' soothed the voice of one of the mentors who had also come to crouch beside us. His hand stroked my shoulders as he tried to calm me down. 'All these boys have done the most terrible things. But they have repented, believe me. They have changed. Look at them. They are not the same people who did those things. Look at them.'

At first I clamped my eyes shut like a stubborn child, but eventually stared at the boys crowding round me with my most menacing scowl. Fear was now more apparent than hope in their expressions, especially in the eyes of the one I had attacked. He was still rubbing his throat as we continued to stare silently at each other. The mentors held a whispered consultation with Brother Bob and Mr. Deed who had come rushing in during the uproar. Finally the leader said, 'Okay, go back to your seats. Samu, continue.'

The boy hesitated, blinking nervously.

'I said, carry on, Samu,' the leader repeated and the boy reluctantly got to his feet.

He began his testimony in a low raspy voice and like previous speakers, had difficulty speaking the local dialect; but I understood him well enough.

We had returned to the bench and it was now Brother Bob who had an arm around my shoulders as the boy's testimony unfolded. I couldn't help shuddering from time to time as I listened, especially when he mentioned having to eat raw worms and lizards, rats and snakes and how the commanders gave them capsules before they went on raids to make them fearless and without conscience. From time to time, Brother Bob muttered in my ear, 'Small brother, it could have been you. But for God's grace, it could have been you.'

But why didn't he run away? I asked myself.

As if he had heard the question, the boy lifted his T-shirt to show us more raised and shiny scars - the letters PRA carved upon his chest. I shuddered again.

'Many times I wanted to run away,' he continued. 'Many, many times, but my sister was also in the camp and the commanders were very wicked. They had no mercy when they caught anyone who tried to run away. And I was afraid that if people saw PRA on my chest they would kill me… I did not think anyone would have time to notice this mark on my forehead.'

I detected a hint of pride as he added, 'We were always very fast in our attacks. In the end, I decided to take a chance because my sister was dead and I wanted to leave that life.'

He wound up his story, glanced in my direction, hesitated, then went slowly back to his seat.

'Small brother, forgive him,' Brother Bob muttered. 'It is hard, I know, but he was not to blame. Can't you see that?'

Confused and shaken as I was by all that I had seen and heard and *done* that afternoon, I no longer knew how I felt. Something seemed to give way inside me and tears filled my eyes, but they didn't fall, thank God! The assembly broke up soon after that, the boys dispersed, and I went forward to apologize to the mentors for causing such a disgraceful disturbance. I thought it was kind of the one who seemed to be the leader of the mentors to say, 'We understand. We truly understand, but believe me, the boy you saw today is not the same person who killed your parents. Only his outer body is the same - not his heart.'

I nodded, but remained far from convinced.

Brother Bob and I had little to say to each other on the long journey home, but before we parted, he asked when we planned to hold the first meeting of LIP, and promised to be there. His gentle tone, like someone visiting a house in mourning, made me realise how much he sympathised with the turmoil churning up my mind. He is a special person - another of my angels.

10 August 1997

To Confession having had time to reflect, but did my penance only half-heartedly. These days, religious duties have very little meaning for me, but for Mams's sake, I shall continue for now.

Full moon tonight and I remember Mr. Danso. Gramma Cobola says he had to be put in the mental hospital after the way the PRA killed his sister and tortured him, otherwise he would have been serenading us with hymns by now in spite of the rain. Poor man! I miss his croaky voice.

18 September 1997

Another busy time during break, recruiting members for LIP. The response has been encouraging, so we hope for a good turnout at the inauguration. Brother Bob is going to try to get the YWCA hall for us. Jogolo and some other teachers have promised to come after seeing our constitution and listening to our plans. Jogolo nodded approvingly when I told him that in the long holidays we plan to undertake projects to raise money for improving the environment and hold literacy classes for young people who have had no opportunity to go to school. He smiled and said, 'I can see you are going to be too busy to get into any mischief. Very good. But don't forget your first priority - getting good 'A' levels.' I am starting to feel a bit excited, as if my blood is flowing again at the rate it used to before Feb.27.

20 September 1997

Chico and Solade helped me sweep the fire debris from our - my - burnt-out house and tidy the yard which I couldn't face doing before now. The place doesn't look so desolate any more. By God's grace, one day I shall build the house of my dreams on that same spot.

I've decided to find another place to stay away from George Town. Don't know how Gramma Cobola will take it, but it's time to move on and not keep reminding myself of the most terrible day in my life. Besides, I need more private space and a table where I can study. I shall tell her tomorrow. No point postponing it. The end of October is my deadline. Hope I find a place I like by then.

Chapter Eighteen

SAMU'S CHOICE

The encounter with the wild-eyed young man shook Samu to the tips of his fingers and toes. Those eyes, those eyes, glaring at him with such fury; and those hands, gripping his throat harder than the vice he had clamped to a piece of wood that morning. He had no doubt that, but for the intervention of the mentors, the young man would have killed him. After his crazy attack, the young man had continued to look at him with hatred, even after he had given his testimony explaining everything. Was that what life outside the camp was going to be like? Samu asked himself. People treating him as if he were a big black snake the moment they found out about his past? If that was the case, the mentors were not telling the truth when they said former rebels could return to ordinary life after their training. So what was the use of learning a trade? Who would give him work once they knew he had been with the PRA? And even if he could start his own carpentry shop, who would come to him as clients? Remembering the lives and property the PRA had destroyed, he could understand how people would want to have their revenge or to keep their distance. Nevertheless, the prospect of having to face such deep hostility undermined his determination to change his way of life and he began seriously to consider returning to the bush where he would be among people in a similar situation.

In the end, it was one small event that made him decide to leave the camp - his failure to complete a wooden bench he had been working on for days. The legs were the problem. No matter how carefully he measured the wood and planed it, he could not make the bench stand squarely on the floor. He kept making adjustments until, losing patience at last, he tossed the legs aside. After a few moments, he picked up one of them again and pretended to work; but when the supervisor's back was turned, snatched up a nail-cutting tool and hid it in the waistband of his shorts.

The actual escape presented no difficulty for someone as accustomed as he to moving stealthily. Creeping half naked out of the dormitory in the middle of the night, he simply waited for the guards on patrol to move to the far side of the compound, then cut the wire fence with the stolen nail cutter and bent the severed pieces over to make a hole large enough for his body to pass through. Within minutes he was moving rapidly through the scrub and savannah grass in the vicinity with practised ease. By daybreak, his movements well concealed by thicker bush, he had already covered three of the twenty or so miles he estimated would take him back to the forest reserve where he hoped his comrades were still lying low.

Several months had passed since he last saw them, but the plan had been to remain there until things quietened down since raids on urban villages yielded richer pickings than those on villages up-country. No doubt, his comrades would regard him with suspicion after his sudden disappearance, but he had prepared his story. He was going to tell them that he had been captured by government soldiers the day he failed to return from that last raid, and that it was only after several unsuccessful attempts that he finally managed to escape.

It was late afternoon by the time he entered the forest reserve. He began to move faster, knowing he was only a few miles from his destination - one of the PRA hideouts fortunate enough to have escaped being bombed by enemy jets. He started seeing signs of human life - a cigarette butt here, a rag there, a spent bullet, a small heap of dried faeces. He had just picked up a damaged part of an RPG launcher when he caught sight of four girls collecting firewood. Having participated in the raids in which they were abducted, he recognised them all.

<><><><><>

The mentors had been right when they told Emmanuel that Samu was no longer the boy who killed his parents in cold blood. Months without using drugs, without hearing or using harsh and vulgar language, of being made to behave politely to everyone, and of being treated with respect and kindness himself, had worked a remarkable transformation of his mind since the day he presented himself at the camp to lay down his arms. As a PRA fighter, he had successfully hardened his heart towards his victims. Now, the sight of the four girls moving about so listlessly, touched his gentler heart. One of the girls was pregnant, he observed - a shaming reminder of the rapes he had joined in before deserting the PRA, and also of his sister, Mawa, who had suffered terrible abuse at the hands of Odinga only to die before she had a chance to live. Recognising and repenting of past crimes had come fairly easily to Samu and guilt washed over him again like a bucket of filthy water. It made him say to himself, let me help these ones, at least.

He scouted the immediate surroundings for a few minutes then, having satisfied himself of the absence of guards, whistled softly through his teeth, 'Psss…'

The frailest-looking of the girls raised her head like a startled antelope and looked around nervously. She had always reminded him of the wading birds that frequented the shallows of the river where he used to fish in a happier time.

'Don't be afraid,' he whispered, emerging from the bushes. 'Come with me. I want to help you.'

The girls also recognised Samu at once, for who could forget that scar? But they also remembered that he had disappeared from the camp some months earlier. And he looked very different now - much cleaner and not as rough as the others even though he was half naked with roughened hair, and leaves stuck to his skin here and there. Besides, his expression seemed genuinely friendly. Desperate to escape the hell their lives had been since their abduction, they needed no great persuasion to abandon their bundles of wood and follow him.

Samu knew this part of the forest well, having explored the area many times before the attack on Sewa City. He moved even faster than before, knowing that when darkness approached and the girls failed to return, a search party would be sent after them. As the precious hours passed, the girls struggled to keep up with him. Granite stones dug into their feet, while tangled vegetation lashed their legs and arms and slapped their faces; but well aware that this might be their only chance to escape, they suffered the discomfort in silence.

The trees and thick undergrowth were beginning to thin out at last when Samu suddenly stopped in his tracks, holding up his hand.

'Wait,' he whispered. 'I hear something.'

It was a sound he knew well - a bird call that could not possibly have been made by any feathered creature. Making a quick decision, he said to the girls, 'Keep going in this direction and you will soon come to a town. It's not far, but go as fast as you can.'

Before they could thank him, Samu had disappeared.

To divert attention away from the girls, he moved in the direction of the bird call with a deliberate lack of caution and not long afterwards, the expected challenge came.

'Who is that?'

'It's me, Samu - Small Leopard,' he added, for having recognised Lans's voice, he hoped using that nickname would influence his fellow spy in his favour. 'I am returning...'

He was still feeling fairly confident that he would be able to talk his way out of trouble as Lans, followed by three other fighters, emerged from the shadows, rifle at the ready and pointing straight at him.

'So…Our Small Leopard has decided to come back …' Lans sneered.

A familiar alteration in his voice made Samu realise at once that his comrade was drugged to his eyeballs and therefore capable of doing anything. Samu's heart started beating hard but he tried not to show that he was afraid.

'What brought Small Leopard back?' Lans continued in the same mocking tone, 'Could it be that when the rainy season ended he remembered that he was a man and no longer a baby? Or,' he went on with added malice, 'has he come to spy on us for those fucking bastards who call themselves the security forces?'

Forcing a careless laugh to show how ridiculous he considered both accusations, Samu started to explain his disappearance; but Lans gave him no time to complete even one sentence before cutting in with, 'We have no use for cowards like you in the PRA, you hear? We don't want your kind. We don't need your kind.' With each sentence, he took a step forward, jerking his rifle in Samu's direction.

Truly frightened now, Samu wondered frantically how he could escape; but there was no time to try anything, for in a move so sudden that even the other fighters let out exclamations of shock, Lans shot him, heaping foul abuse upon his mother as he did so.

The bullet tore into Samu, severing his aorta. With a gasping cry, he instinctively covered the burning, gaping wound with both arms in the vain hope of preventing his life-blood from escaping; but it gushed out relentlessly. Still crying out, he swayed on his feet for a moment before falling to his knees and collapsing sideways.

The crack of gunshot and the piercing human cries roused a troop of monkeys which had spent the night in branches high overhead. They called out to one another in alarm and were still jabbering away when Samu's heart stopped beating. Lans kicked his body aside and the search party continued on its way. They tracked the passage of the girls to the edge of the forest before coming to the conclusion that, against the odds, they had somehow managed to escape.

Chapter Nineteen

MIRACLES DO HAPPEN

6 October 1997

Yesterday was another one of those days that will remain etched on my mind forever. We spent the whole morning at the YWCA hall preparing for the launching of LIP. Chico made a large banner with LOVE IS POWER painted in the national colours - so striking that we congratulated him.

Our recruiting efforts produced a good harvest - more than 200 people showed up - almost every secondary school in the city was represented; some students from the university and the teacher-training college also came.

Brother Bob and one of the Muslim students joined *les copains* on stage and led opening prayers. Afterwards Chico, chairman for the occasion, made a short speech stating the purpose of the meeting before inviting me to speak. Literary and Debating Society experience stood me in good stead, but still, never having addressed such a large audience before, stage-fright threatened as I rose to my feet and saw all those expectant faces raised towards me. It was a sense of invisible forms nodding approval that stopped the butterflies in my stomach and strengthened my voice as I began to talk about my dream and what followed.

I'm sure public speakers and actors always know when they have captured their audience, because *I* could feel positive vibes flowing towards me. It made me so excited that I put down my notes and simply allowed the words to flow.

'So, future members of LIP,' I said, adding, 'and I hope that will be true after today. If we want a better country, we have to start by acting differently towards each other. No matter what part of the country we come from and no matter what our status in life, we have to respect each other, not fight each other, or compete with each other in harmful ways. We have to build each other up, not pull each other down. At this critical time in our country's history, we have to be prepared to let bygones be bygones and start afresh. That is what LIP is all about - love in action, because...'

Suddenly remembering a documentary I had seen of Ghana's independence day, I raised my arms in the air and shouted, 'LOVE IS POWER!', gesturing to the audience to repeat the slogan with me.

'LOVE IS POWER!' they shouted back, and rose to their feet, applauding. I couldn't believe it. They seemed to be applauding *me*.

Brother Bob leaned across the table to say, '*You* are a born politician.'

'I beg you, not a politician,' I replied, but all the same, felt dizzy with delight.

To crown it all, a lone voice began the chorus of what had become my favourite Bob Marley song: '*One love, one heart...*'

Those of us who knew it, and it turned out that there were many in the audience, promptly joined in, clapping our hands and clicking our fingers to maintain the rhythm.

'*Let's get together and feel all right.*'

How appropriate! I thought, deeply satisfied with the proceedings. We sang the chorus again and again till the whole room seemed to pulsate with energy. Those of us on the stage turned to each other grinning, and spontaneously embraced.

What brought me down to earth again was the news Brother Bob gave me as we walked away from the hall.

'I went back to the camp the other day,' he said. 'That boy you wanted to kill - Samu - he has disappeared.'

'Disappeared!' I said, 'You mean he's run away?'

'It seems so. Nobody has seen him and the guards found a gaping hole in the fence... They can't understand it because he was apparently getting on very well - learning carpentry and all. '

'Could he have gone back to the PRA?' I asked since that has been known to happen.

'Somehow, I doubt it,' he said. 'I won't forget his face when he had finished his testimony. I think he really wanted to be finished with that terrible life...'

I thought no more about Samu because when I got home, even

more arresting news was awaiting my arrival.

Modu had been washing plates at the stand-pipe. The moment he heard Whisky's friendly bark, he straightened up, grinning from ear to ear, and announced that Hamida had returned.

My heart must have stopped for a couple of seconds. All the papers I was carrying fell to the ground and scattered.

'What! Wh..When? I stuttered. 'What happened?'

I am quite fond of Modu, but I came close to punching him with vexation when he told me that he didn't know because it happened when he went down to the petrol station to buy kero. He'd only heard a passer-by calling out to Gramma Cobola to ask whether she saw Pa Noah's daughter being taken to the junction to look for transport.

Throwing him a look of intense irritation, I left him to pick up my papers, while I took the back stairs in two leaps and ran into the house where Gramma Cobola, groaning a little, was just rising from her seat on her front porch. She had been doing her embroidery as usual.

Trying to contain my agitation, since no one was supposed to know that my interest in Hamida was more than the normal concern of one neighbour for another, I said, 'Gramma, is it true that Hamida Noah has returned?'

'It's true,' she replied, forgetting her aches and pains for the moment. 'God does not sleep-oh, Manny. I know many of you young people don't believe that, but God does *not* asleep. *I* always had faith that the girl would come back. The people at the top end brought four of them down the road. They said the girls just appeared this morning with a strange story. They have taken Hamida to her people in town.'

'How was she, ma? How did she look?' I asked, though I was afraid to hear the answer.

Gramma Cobola must have heard an anxious tremor in my voice because she gave me a sharp look before telling me that she'd heard that Hamida was as thin as a rope and refusing to speak, but her belly was flat, for which we should all thank God.

Feeling as if I'd been punched in the gut, I quickly excused myself. These days, nobody opens their door to unexpected visitors after dark, otherwise I would have gone straight to the Noahs' place. Instead,

I lay on my narrow bed tormenting myself with anxious thoughts of the 'what if' variety. Supper was fried fish and boiled plantain, one of my favourites, but I ate without tasting a thing. And I didn't sleep much either.

Straight after Mass today, I went to the Noahs' place but didn't see Hamida. Pa Noah said she was resting. I felt both disappointed and relieved. I asked how she escaped but Pa Noah said that they didn't know the full story yet because she hadn't said a word since she came back.

'From what we have heard,' he told me, 'it seems that one of the rebels helped them, but I find that hard to believe.'

I also found that hard to believe; but on my way home, I remembered the missing boy and wondered briefly whether the two events could possibly be connected. I dismissed the idea, though, thinking that the camp was too far from the forest behind George Town for that to be likely.

Chapter Twenty

HAMIDA

9 October 1997

Moved to my new address after school - one room on the ground floor of a house which is nearer to St. Peter's, and modern. I'm so glad Gramma Cobola didn't make me feel guilty about leaving her. This is just what I need - a bed, chair and table, a string for hanging up my clothes and a small porch where I can cook. I have to share the bathroom and toilet with the man who lives on the other side. Not too keen on sharing with a perfect stranger, but it will be good practice for going to university. I have to buy a small kerosene stove and a kettle, with pots, plates, cups and cutlery, etc. etc. Hmm. This month my allowance from Uncle Eku will barely be enough.

Took assembly this a.m. Went to Jogolo's office afterwards to return the hymnbook and Bible and his copy of 'The Daily Nation' caught my eye. Big black headlines: FORMER REBEL DIES RESCUING SCHOOLGIRLS. I only had time to read 'Fawzia, Becklyn, Rhoda and Amina (*their real names are withheld*)…' when I heard Jogolo's footsteps returning. I suspected that the article was about Hamida's escape and could hardly wait for the end of school so I could get my own copy from the paper boys at the petrol station.

The article said the girls had been abducted after the attack on Sewa City and taken to a rebel hideout deep in the forest reserve, but actually located only a few miles outside the province. They had suffered the usual fate of girls captured by the PRA and at least one of them was thought to be carrying a child fathered by one of the 'miscreants.' Apparently they were sent to look for firewood and met a boy who used to be a rebel but had left the PRA some months before. He offered to help them escape and led them through the forest - a difficult journey taking several hours - till they arrived somewhere near George Town. Just before they reached the outskirts of the village, the boy heard a suspicious noise and, taking no chances, quickly pointed the way out of the forest to the girls, told them to run as fast as they could, then set off in another direction. Not very long afterwards, the girls heard a gunshot followed by some loud cries, then nothing. The report ended, 'The girls believe that their rescuer might have been killed by his former comrades at arms, though they do not know why. If that was the case, may God have mercy on his soul for his good deed at the last.'

I feel so frustrated that I can't ask Hamida for more details. Pa Noah always tells me that she's 'resting' when I go to their place. I don't believe him, but what can I do?

20 October 1997

Passed by the Noahs this evening after going to Confession. Pa Noah must have been feeling really desperate because he allowed me to see Hamida at last, saying, 'I don't know what else to do, Manny. She refuses to see a doctor, and I can't force her. When I called one, she locked herself in her room. I have tried our own way, but they tell me that it is her mother who has to do this and do that. What can my wife do? I don't know…*you* are her age group and she has known you since she was a child. Maybe she will talk to you.'

Hamida took a long time to emerge. By the time she came from behind the curtain that conceals the private section of their present home, my heart was pounding so hard that I felt a bit sick. I had been thinking: suppose she won't come; suppose she comes but refuses to speak even to me; and most worrying, suppose *I* can't face her.

I had to bite my lip to stop myself from breaking down when a shadow of Hamida's former self finally appeared. Her cheeks have almost disappeared and her complexion, so perfect before, is as pale as a corpse - almost grey - and rough with pimples, as if she hasn't seen sunshine since they captured her. Her arms and legs are like sticks, criss-crossed with scratches. So many blades of grass and thorns must have torn her skin when she was carrying out her slave labour. Ah! Ah!

She came right up to me weeping, her head bowed, her hands covering her face. For several moments she neither raised her head nor spoke - just stood there as if *she* had committed a crime and was waiting for her punishment. That was when I realised that I loved her as much as ever - even more perhaps, though I didn't know whether it was like a brother again or what. The only thing I knew for certain was that I was glad I hadn't gone to America.

I completely forgot that Pa Noah was in the parlour. Not that it would have made any difference. I put my arms gently round Hamida's fragile shoulders and drew her to me. She stood there like a plank and continued to weep in huge gasps, just like Florrie used to when she fell and hurt herself.

'Manny,' she sobbed, her voice muffled by my shoulder. 'Manny, I am so…so ugly and…and I feel so…so dirty.'

Not knowing what to say, and feeling as if my heart would break, I only held her more tightly.

When she finally pulled away, I tilted her chin towards me and whispered through my tears, 'I shall come again tomorrow. Okay?'

For several seconds, she stared into my eyes as if she couldn't believe that I hadn't found her repulsive, then turned and walked away.

Pa Noah had been there all along. When we were alone again, he said to me, tears glistening in his one good eye, 'You see my trouble? I don't know what to do… But at least she spoke.'

I can think of only one person who might be able to advise us sensibly - Brother Bob. I shall go and see him tomorrow.

Ah, Hamida! But I thank God she survived.

21 October 1997

I went straight to the Church of the Master this a.m. to look for Brother Bob. Broke down completely when I started telling him about Hamida's pitiful state. Very embarrassing, but I couldn't help it. Afterwards he made me pray with him, then looked at me for a long time before saying,

'Small brother, from what you have told me, what that girl needs above everything else is for her self-esteem to be restored. As her boyfriend, you are one of the best people to do that, but for that same reason you might find it very hard. You know what I mean? No man likes to think his woman has been, you know… um… intimate with another man, let alone a disgusting, perhaps diseased person. And in this case, she might have been forced to sleep with more than one such person. Seriously, small brother, do you think you can handle it, especially when you've been through so much yourself? I am not saying withdraw your friendship - that would be very wrong - but perhaps it would be better for you not to go to her house too often. She's not really your responsibility, you know.'

Brother Bob put into words some of the very thoughts that came to me while I lay awake last night. I told him the conclusion I came to - that I wouldn't be able to look at myself in the mirror if I didn't do what I could to help Hamida. That her mother is helpless, her father confused and besides, I loved her like a sister long before I fell in love with her. Also that Khalid was my very best friend.

He gave me another long and searching look before saying, 'Then I shall pray for all of you every day. As my Master said, with God *all* things, not some-oh…*all* things are possible…'

Thanks to Brother Bob, Pa Noah and I now have a plan of action. 1. Complete medical check-up on Monday, including blood tests for STDs and HIV (God forbid!). 2. Start rape counselling at Red Cross post-trauma clinic (Brother Bob will arrange it and let us know). 3.Tender Loving Care. 4.TLC 5.TLC and the same for 6 and 7 and 8, etc. etc. etc.

Chapter Twenty-one

A QUIET MUTINY

'L-C Leopard, this is *too* much now,' Brigadier Cobra had remarked as the two commanders listened to reports on the BBC about atrocities in the capital and the surrounding villages in the aftermath of the PRA attack.

'Yes, it is very bad,' agreed Leopard who had been listening to the broadcast with equal disgust. 'It is 'Operation no mercy' all over again. Who will support the PRA after this?'

'Only people who don't think for themselves and those who are benefiting from the confusion in the country - people like that Papa's friend - the one who flies in and out of here all the time. No one can tell me that *he* is helping the PRA because he believes in our revolution…'

'He is in it for the diamonds, that's all,' Leopard agreed. 'Brigadier… don't you think it is time for us to do something?'

Leopard's suggestion had increased the turmoil in Cobra's mind to the extent that he only noticed that he had come to the end of the cigarette he was smoking when hot ash burned his fingertips. Mumbling a curse, he dropped the smouldering butt and crushed it into the ground. He agreed that they needed to do something to save the PRA, though the thought of a confrontation with Kanekeh started the now familiar burning in his stomach.

'Let us bide our time and see what Papa is going to do next,' he said. 'Maybe he himself will realise that he is not going to win this war. In any case, I don't want to challenge him until I know we will succeed.'

Strongly suspecting that Brigadier Cobra's hesitation was due more to diffidence than prudence, Leopard reminded him that Odinga, Mamba, Pele and Ironbone, who would probably have supported Kanekeh to the bitter end, had perished in the battle for the capital, Fela and Dragon were out of the way at Camp Justice and the whereabouts of Rambo and at least a hundred fighters remained unknown.

'Now that Odinga and the others are no more,' he said, 'why don't we start working on Ninja? Let us grumble about the war when he is around so we can find out how he feels about it. Perhaps he is feeling just like us.'

'Or he might pretend to be feeling the same, then go and tell Papa what we have been saying,' Cobra warned.

'Not if we are smart,' Leopard said. 'Let us praise the Pa to the sky and put all the blame for what happened in the city on undisciplined fighters and the government soldiers who only joined us recently. After what happened before the last 'Operation no mercy', Ninja already knows what we think of this kind of wickedness towards innocent people, so he won't be afraid to confide in us…'

'You are right,' said Cobra beginning to warm to the suggestion. 'And I think the others in Camp Justice will support us if they know that Kanekeh is no longer in control. They too must be feeling tired by now…Yes, it's a good idea. If things seem to be going according to plan, we can send a secret message to the MRC via those Red Cross people to say we want to negotiate peace.'

'I am sure the answer will be favourable,' said Leopard, his eyes sparkling happily now that Cobra seemed as enthusiastic as he. 'This war is not going in anybody's favour. How long are we going to continue fighting?'

Kanekeh's subsequent actions strengthened Cobra's resolve to carry out their plan, for ending the war seemed to be the last thing on the PRA leader's mind. Having satisfied himself, through radio reports, that the foreign troops were confining their operations to securing Sewa City and the areas around it, his new strategy was to continue harassing the government by ordering sudden raids on villages and towns in the more insecure parts of the country. What he did not realise until the PRA had suffered some unexpected defeats, was that the MRC had embarked on a new strategy of their own by providing the local militia, which had sprung up everywhere, with guns and ammunition, and even basic training to fight on the government side.

For the third time in his campaign, Kanekeh found himself outmanoeuvred. Instead of the helpless villagers they were used to, his fighters found themselves having to battle against a well armed and determined enemy and to do so without many of their most experienced fighters. However, convinced that the MRC would not be foolish enough to bring back ' Security Solutions', Kanekeh remained confident that with his control of the diamond fields unchallenged so far, he would soon be able to rebuild his forces. It therefore came as a complete shock when one of his guards ushered in a trembling child fighter one evening saying Captain Ninja had sent him with an urgent message.

'Shi…it!' Kanekeh roared, when the boy fearfully whispered the message in his ear. Springing to his feet, he almost knocked the boy over and pushed aside his woman who had come running to the room at the sound of his enraged bellow. Blood rushed to his head, threatening to burst a vein. He was breathing hard as he stamped out of his quarters. Ignoring the guards who had jumped to attention when he appeared at the door, he ordered his driver to take him to the town council building which the commanders used for relaxation.

'Brigadier Cobra,' he demanded, charging into the room, his brow like a thundercloud. 'What is this I am hearing?'

Out of sheer habit, Cobra jumped to his feet with his usual deference, his heart thudding like muffled drumbeats, his stomach on fire. So Ninja had betrayed them after all. To give himself time to regain his composure, he stammered, 'Wh…what, sah?'

'That you and L-C Leopard are negotiating peace with the MRC. Is it true?'

Cobra glanced at Leopard, who urged him with a look not to lose his nerve, before fixing Ninja with a menacing stare.

Cobra took a deep breath to control his churning stomach before replying.

'Yessah,' he said. 'We contacted the MRC because we thought it was time to end this war. The bloodshed has been going on for nearly five years now, nobody is winning and the people are suffering too much. And we too are tired of fighting.'

For several seconds Kanekeh looked from Cobra to Leopard in speechless fury then, overcome by his emotions, he bellowed, 'Behind my back, you cowards? Behind my back!'

'No Papa, we are not cowards,' Leopard interjected with a calmness that sharpened the insubordination he intended to convey.

'You should know that by now.'

'What are you then, enh?...Traitors. Bloody traitors! I should have dealt with the two of you that day. Bastards and children of bastards! I spit on your mothers! At least there is one decent one among you. Captain Ninja, arrest these men.'

'No, sah,' Ninja replied, causing an even nastier shock to Kanekeh's system, as well as joyful astonishment to Cobra and Leopard. 'I am with them, and so are most of the fighters. The only thing we did not agree about was keeping our decision a secret from you. I did not want you to hear about it on the radio...'

'Papa, please listen to what we have to say,' Cobra interrupted hurriedly. 'We have asked for amnesty for all of us in exchange for laying down our arms. We have also asked for you and one or two others to have a place in the government. The MRC say they are considering the matter...'

This information did nothing to appease Kanekeh who continued to regard them with the utmost contempt.

'How can you deal with such criminals?' he said. 'Do you think I started the PRA to sit down at the same table with dogs? We have suffered defeats before, but did we not regain everything we lost? We can do it again. In any case, as soon as you lay down your arms, they will arrest you. You can't believe anything those people say...'

Cobra made one final attempt to persuade Kanekeh at least to wait for a further response from the MRC, but all to no avail. Taking another aggressive step forward, he threw up his arms, shouting, 'Go to hell! You people have nothing to tell me that I want to hear.'

With that, he turned on his heel and stamped out of the room, leaving the three commanders feeling stunned and slightly ashamed, though no less determined to continue their negotiations with the MRC. They could have arrested Kanekeh, but had already come to a unanimous decision that for the sake of the high esteem in which they once held him, they would allow him to escape - if that was his choice.

Still boiling with anger at their betrayal, Kanekeh considered his immediate position as the Land Rover rocked and rolled its way back to his quarters. He had no doubt that Ninja had told the truth when he said they had the support of the majority of the fighters stationed in Dembu. He would not dare lie about something so easily disproved. There remained the fighters at Camp Justice, but even if he could count on the loyalty of those commanders, they were too far away to be able to intervene urgently on his behalf. All things considered, wisdom counselled that he put distance between himself and Dembu at once, in case the MRC demanded that as part of the peace deal, the commanders hand him over to face trial. Considering his options would have to wait for another day.

Upon reaching his quarters, he ordered the driver to wait in the Land Rover and entered the building as close to running as was consistent with maintaining his dignity.

'Femata, Femata,' he whispered to his woman who was on the porch, anxiously awaiting his return. 'Quick, quick. Go and collect our things. We have to leave now, now.'

Confused and alarmed by the sudden turn of events, Femata wasted several seconds darting aimlessly here and there before heading for the bed-room where Kanekeh had already pulled his pistol from under his pillow and, from under the mattress, a leather pouch full of uncut diamonds.

'Hurry up, hurry up,' he urged when he saw that she had not yet started removing clothes from the rack, then stood over her, barely containing his impatience, as she began to pull various items out of the lopsided chest of drawers, from the rack, from an armchair, and stuffing them into two enormous bags of woven plastic - one red, one green.

'Okay, let us go,' he said when she finally told him she was ready and, having assured himself that they had forgotten nothing important hurried outside, leaving her to struggle with the bags till she reached the porch where one of the guards relieved her of the load.

Without a word to the guards apart from Femata's muttered 'thank you', the fugitives boarded the Land Rover with racing hearts since they had no idea that they were in no immediate danger.

'Take me to that place near the border,' Kanekeh ordered. It was the last time he would use that commanding tone of voice.

Chapter Twenty-two

IMPERFECT PEACE

17 November 1997

I am almost becoming a fixture in the Noahs' house. Spent three hours there after Mass. Pa Noah even offered me lunch. He seems to look forward to my visits, though he has many other callers. I feel for him. So much on his plate. And it must be painful to be living in that tight place after his beautiful, spacious house with a view of the sea.

Brother Bob's plan is working well. Counselling by professionals, iron tablets, antibiotics, multivitamins and TLC have started to take effect. Hamida is looking much better. But today was another of her silent days. After fifteen minutes of introducing different topics of conversation without success, I said in desperation, 'Hamida, do you remember that letter I wrote you last year? The one where I said not even water would ever come between us?'

Slight nod.

'Everything I said is still true, you know,' I went on. 'No matter what has happened, everything is still true.'

'Okay,' she answered as she had before - a lifetime ago, it seems now. I was very disheartened when tears started making tracks down her cheeks again, because I thought she had progressed beyond that weepy stage. Several more silent minutes passed, then she brushed the tears aside and said, 'Manny…in the bush…I became pregnant, but the baby came out… soon after I felt it moving.'

I can't say that information was a shock, but it hurt like hell. It still hurts like hell when I think of it. To comfort her further, I told her again that it made no difference to how I felt about her. I didn't know whether or not I was telling the truth until the words left my lips. Only then did I realise that I still love her with all my heart and all I want in this world is for her to get well again and be able to put her ordeal behind her.

I took her hand. For once she didn't remove it, which I took as a sign of progress despite the tears. I'm also more than grateful that her treatment for STDs has worked and she's in the clear. Two more weeks to go before we know the results of the final HIV test. If *I* am so frightened that I can't even pray, I can't begin to imagine what she and her family are going through.

1 December 1997

There was dancing in the street today after the news that Kelli Kanekeh had fled across the border. Mori Jusu (Also known as Brigadier Cobra, is the new leader of the PRA and Prince Mwamba (also known as Lieutenant-Colonel Leopard) is his deputy. They have sent a long statement to the newspapers apologising for the havoc the PRA has caused in the country. Apparently they have offered to lay down their arms in exchange for amnesty, and the establishment of a government of national unity, with positions for some of the senior commanders. No decision from the MRC as yet. I should feel delighted that they have made the offer, but I don't. Not after all that cruelty and killing and senseless destruction. Even now some of them are still doing it. We heard heavy gunfire again early this morning, always a sign that government soldiers are still trying to flush out PRA fighters hiding in the forest reserve.

4 December 1997

LIP meeting this afternoon. Heated discussion about what people's attitude should be to ex-PRA fighters now that peace negotiations seem to be starting. Most members are not in favour of power-sharing with former rebels, but a few said that we should support whatever promotes peace.Very noble and in keeping with LIP objectives, but it goes against all my instincts. It would be like rewarding them for wrecking the country. Yet if the MRC don't agree, they might go back to the bush and continue their looting and killing and maiming…It's a dilemma-oh.

Dropped in to see Hamida after the meeting and noticed a difference in the atmosphere in the house as soon as I walked in. It was as if the walls were standing upright again after sagging for months. I discovered why when Pa Noah held me by the shoulders and said, his voice throbbing with emotion, 'Manny… Allah is great! The girl seems to be all right. No sign of that terrible sickness. Allah is great!'

It was my turn to sag, so enormous was my relief. Even to my own ears, my voice sounded choked as I replied, 'Praise God.'

'Go and meet her,' Pa Noah said kindly. 'She's ironing in the back.'

Their helper did not come to work today and Hamida was attacking a pile of clothes with such vigour that I felt that with the fear of AIDS removed, she had left the past behind her at last. Thank God, I thought again as she put the goose down on its stand and came towards me, smiling. Not one of her headlight beams of our carefree days, but still a proper smile, showing her perfect teeth. Full of joy at the good news and the sight of her smiling face, I reached for her without thinking. Bad mistake. As if avoiding a wasp, she pulled back abruptly, leaving me feeling stupid.

She gave me a stricken look, the bright promise in her smile extinguished, and returned to her ironing. I realised then that while she's made a lot of progress, full recovery has to remain a hope for the future. We probably don't know half of what she suffered.

'Do you want me to go?' I said.

Hamida shook her head.

'Then leave the ironing for a while and come and sit down,' I told her.

For a few minutes we sat side by side on the back steps in total silence. Hamida bent over, fiddling with the tassels on her slippers while I tried to find something to say that would ease the tension. In the end, it was she who spoke first.

'Manny, I want to thank you from the bottom of my heart.'

'For what ?' I asked.

'For being such a good friend to me. I would not have blamed you if you had been too embarrassed to come near me after, … My other so-called friends have only been here a few times, you know.'

I said, 'How many times do I have to remind you about what I wrote in that letter?'

'So much has happened since then,' she answered, sighing. After a pause, she added, 'Manny, I don't want to be anybody's girlfriend. I…'

She sounded so quietly matter-of-fact that had she not been a Muslim, I would have thought she had already made up her mind to become a nun. Cursing the rebels under my breath, I said as firmly as I could, 'I'm not going to listen to such rubbish. Let's talk about something else.'

She said, 'If you say so, but I mean it-oh.'

That seemed like the right moment to ask her the question that had been nagging at me for weeks.

'That rebel boy who helped you and the other girls to escape, did you have a good look at him?'

'I knew him,' Hamida replied to my greatest surprise. 'We were all in the same camp. He was one of the ones that attacked George Town.'

'What did he look like?' I asked, but all at once knew exactly what her answer would be.

'He had a lo…ong scar right across his forehead,' she replied, using her finger to show me what she meant. 'Like this…'

'I know the one you mean,' I said and made her gasp with astonishment by describing my own encounter with him.

'You!!' she exclaimed wide-eyed, knowing how much I hate a lot of violence. 'Manny, you!!'

Had Hamida not, just minutes before, tried to crush the hope I still cherished that we could somehow turn back time and return to the happy days of year before last, I might have echoed that journalist's prayer. After all, I owed Samu a debt of gratitude for giving her back to us. However, furious all over again at the damage PRA fighters had done to innocent people, I almost rejoiced to know that he might have come to a bloody end. He could be burning in hell, for all I cared.

I really wish I could have Brother Bob's attitude, but I don't. For me, trying to forgive those people is like climbing a steep and rugged hill with very high chances of slipping backwards. I thought I had reached a stage where at least, I no longer wished Samu any harm, yet no sooner did something remind me of his connection with the PRA than I detested him all over again and wanted him to *suffer*. I just have to pray harder to be able to forgive him as well as the others. It would be better for my peace of mind, I know.

As for Hamida, if she thinks I am going to give her up because she says so, she doesn't know Emmanuel Martin. Not unless *I* am convinced that there's no hope.

29 December 1997

The rumour machine is working overtime again. People are saying that the US and UK ambassadors are putting pressure on the MRC to accept the PRA's offer of peace in exchange for amnesty, though Kelli Kanekeh will be tried for war crimes if they ever get their hands on him. I still feel cheated that most of those criminals might go unpunished - more so because today LIP members went to the amputee camp, to see what we could do to help. We had to leave after about half an hour - just couldn't take it. So many heartbreaking sights - a child lighting a cigarette for her father and helping him to smoke it; a little girl not more than seven, buttoning her father's shirt, then feeding him as if *he* was the child; a mother trying to carry her baby, both of them with stumps instead of hands; a young farmer with his arms amputated to the elbows, just sitting there staring into space. Hmm. I hope it will be a bit less upsetting next time we go.

Peace at any price seems to be the name of the game. But what about justice? We can only pray that the PRA leaders have genuinely repented and won't put the country through such hell again - and that people who want power have learned a lesson.

20 January 1998

We had a LIP Executive meeting this p.m. News that a branch opened up-country during Christmas hols - the first one. It seems the word is beginning to spread. Wonderful. I was beginning to feel a bit discouraged. Brother Bob had to remind me to 'Keep the faith.' It's a pity that we'll have to cut down activities till after 'A' levels. Or perhaps not. Members in Lower Sixth and college students who are not in final year could carry on with the literacy classes. I must bring it up at the next meeting.

Dropped in to see Gramma Cobola on the way home. She has

cataracts now, she says, so she can't do embroidery any more; but she seems otherwise the same, camphor smell, 'atritis' and all. Modu is in disgrace and under threat of being sent back to his people for taking small items belonging to Gramma Cobola - to sell, or perhaps he has a girl-friend, she says.

Gramma Cobola said, 'I won't tolerate that-oh. Next thing, my bed sheets and towels will start disappearing one by one. You better talk to him, Manny. He seems to respect you.'

I gave Modu a stern, big brotherly lecture before I left. I hope it works, because if he loses his home with Gramma Cobola, I don't know what will become of him. She says his people have nothing.

She asked in a pointed way, whether I had seen Hamida lately. I was happy to be able to tell her that Hamida is almost like her old self again. Actually, she's looking better than her old self. Suffering seems to have matured her in a beautiful way - especially the expression in her eyes. Even *les copains* have remarked on it. She still doesn't say much, but it's just quietness now, no longer that depression, thank God.

17 February 1998

Brother Bob got married again this a.m. to a pleasant, soft-spoken lady with a small middle and a shapely behind. Didn't even know he had a new woman. Small wedding at his church. Overheard one of the women behind me gossiping to the other, 'But don't you think it is too soon after Hortense died?' Come to think about it, it does seem a bit soon, but then the man must have been lonely and, being so godly and a pastor as well, he didn't want to sin. Anyway, that is his business and these are not normal times. Very pleased for him. If anyone deserves to be happy, it's Brother Bob.

18 April 1998

My nineteenth birthday. Only one present - from Hamida, another Wilbur Smith novel and a beautiful card, though just a friendly message on it. Felt so sad that Mams and Dad were not here to celebrate it with me. I bought myself a cheap radio as a birthday present from Uncle Eku. First thing I heard was that a new Electoral Commission has been appointed, which means we're moving toward elections as promised in the peace deal people are talking about. Good news! Also, the present foreign troops are going to be replaced by Blue Berets under the United Nations flag to keep the peace. *Please* God, keep the country quiet, so we can do our 'A' levels. I'm *so* tired of school.

25 April 1998

Jogolo called us to his office one by one to talk about the future - careers, etc. I can't decide yet, but I'm leaning towards teaching to begin with - I like to influence people. He is applying for scholarships to the university for some of us. I must get down to serious revision as from tomorrow, so no more diary till 'A' levels are over.

9 September 1998

I remember Mammy B. saying, 'Avoid overused words and phrases in your essays. That is one of the practices that give good marks in English exams.' I usually try to follow her advice, but sometimes I can't think of a better way of expressing something than with an overused word or a platitude like 'Time is a great healer'. Hmm. I wonder whether Mammy B. will ever return. This country has lost a good teacher. Pity.

Indeed, time is a great healer. Hamida came to a LIP meeting with me today and stood up confidently to ask an intelligent question after Professor Samba's interesting talk. It was about how to avoid conflict situations in the community. So proud of my brave girl. When we got back to their place, I slipped my arm around her waist and gave it a squeeze before we parted. She gave me one of her wary looks but didn't stiffen or remove my hand, so hope is rising again. She's promised to come and cook for me one day soon as a 'going-to-university present.' At least she trusts me that much. Another promising sign.

10 September 1998

'A' level results. Quite disappointed but not surprised to get only C in French. Too many other things on my mind. Bs in English and Economics. *Les copains* didn't do much better. Our results are not at all bad, considering, but I'm sure Jogolo is disappointed. At least my university place is secure - except for the scholarship. Why are they taking so lo…oong to decide, I wonder. Please God, let me get it! *Please.*

22 September 1998

The best news today. Full scholarship - tuition, books, board and lodging. Thank God. Must call Uncle Eku tomorrow to tell him. I can now start getting ready for college with my mind at rest. Hmm. I wonder what the next four years hold in store for me and for the country. After what happened, I shall never stop expecting the unexpected.

30 September 1998

As she promised, Hamida came to cook for me after going to market herself - groundnut soup - finger-licking delicious even without pig's feet which, like a good Muslim, she refuses to touch. Pa Noah must also trust me to have allowed her to come. On the other hand, I suppose that, as far as he's concerned, the worst that could happen has already happened; and she's probably told him about her 'no boyfriend' decision. They've become very close now that she can't have proper conversations with Mama Abi.

From what happened today, I'm feeling more and more optimistic that her 'no boyfriend' attitude is dying a natural death. After we had eaten, she came to sit with me on the bed without any persuasion, though she had sat on the chair before. In a little while, she brought her legs up and curled up beside me while we talked about Khalid and the fun we used to have in better times. It was a bitter-sweet conversation which made us both a bit tearful. Conversation dried up after a while and I must have dozed off. Woke with a start to find Hamida curled up tighter beside me - just like pictures of a foetus in a womb - and sound asleep. I fitted my body round hers. She stirred and murmured and sighed, but didn't move away or change position. Things started happening, but given no encouragement, subsided after a while and I was content to hold her close and feel her breathing.

She removed my arm when she woke up, but there was no rejection or indifference in the gesture; only a kind of familiarity, as if it was something she had done many times before, and would do many times again. For the first time in ages, I felt at peace with myself as I accompanied her home.

I don't know why, but I have a strong feeling that Dad is nearby as I'm writing this. I can almost hear him saying, 'Manny, don't forget what I told you about 'doing it.' Are you prepared?'

Ah, I miss him! I miss him-oh. I miss him. And Mams too. What else would they like to know, I wonder. Well, Dad and Mams, your son is all right - more or less. I've been trying to get on with life, thanks mainly to Uncle Eku and to a wonderful new friend - a pastor everybody calls Brother Bob. I passed my 'A' levels and won a full scholarship to the university. And I am trying to make things better in the country in my own small way. Oh, yes, and your son is in love - deeply. You know the girl - Pa Noah's daughter, Hamida. My hopes are high that winning her is just a matter of time. And no, Dad, I haven't forgotten what you told me. You can rest in perfect peace.

EPILOGUE

From its hillside perch, the mansion enjoyed a panoramic view of the Atlantic Ocean, now darkening after a spectacular sunset. However, nature's glory made no impression on the two men sitting at a table on the wide veranda. With their drinks in tall glasses hardly touched, they were engaged in a gloomy conversation, for their great venture had come to an abrupt and humiliating end.

In the nearly five years it lasted, Pablo Malick had grown enormously stout - a man-mountain, one might say. Even the capacious gown he had on could not conceal the considerable mound his belly made as he slouched in his chair, thighs splayed. By contrast, Kelli Kanekeh, still looked remarkably fit for his age; only his eyes told a different story, revealing as they did, weariness, uncertainty and inner torment.

'My brother, try to look on the good side of things,' Malick said, making no attempt to hide his growing irritation. 'After all, you fulfilled one of your own dreams - your enemies ran away. What am *I* to say?'

He knew he should be feeling more sympathetic towards his friend and former partner. After all, Kanekeh could hardly be blamed for his commanders' decision to give up their struggle against the government. Once those foreign troops entered the picture with their superior firepower, seasoned fighters and jet bombers, the PRA's chances of winning the war receded faster than an ebbing tide. Yet facing the wreckage of his hopes had been like being forced to chew handfuls of bitter cola. He felt completely let down and would have preferred not to have to see, let alone talk to Kanekeh before coming to terms with his own gnawing sense of failure. In the end, the man had brought him nothing but embarrassment and heavy financial losses.

'Yes, they ran away,' Kanekeh conceded, 'but not in the way I wanted it to happen. I wanted to be the one to kick them out. And I wanted to look right into their eyes, so they would know that *I* was the one who did it. I, Kelli Kanekeh, the man they put in jail for nothing.'

'I can understand that,' Malick replied. 'But still, from what people say, some of them are suffering now, just as you wanted them to suffer - the ex-president most of all. His kidneys have packed up. They say it is only a machine that is keeping him alive.'

Kanekeh's immediate response to this news was, 'Serves the bastard right. But,' he went on to tell Malick, 'you know, in the end, kicking him out was not the main reason I started the PRA. I really wanted to change our country for the better…'

Malick's massive shoulders moved in an indifferent shrug.

'Ah, well,' he said, 'you know that the outcome of every undertaking is in Allah's hands. As I say, look on the good side. At least you have managed to escape with your life. Those boys could have decided to kill you, you know. Or you could have been facing a trial for war crimes. You have not lost money, because you did not have money in the first place; and if you have lost face, it's only with your own countrymen. In any case, most of them have never seen your face or heard your voice. *I* have personally lost millions of dollars supporting the PRA. Millions. And as for the people I persuaded to invest in the project, I am even afraid to face some of them now.'

Further depressed by this reminder of his failure to fulfil, not only his own mission, but also his part in what was after all a business deal, Kanekeh fixed his brooding, bloodshot gaze on the puddle of condensation wetting the table round his glass. To think that PRA commanders - his boys - were actively pursuing peace with those corrupt and useless soldiers now in power - bargaining for positions in a so-called government of national unity whereas he, the founder of such a noble movement, could expect nothing but further disgrace and worse if he showed his face in the country again. Why did God forsake me like this, he wondered in confused resentment. Why? Why? I had only good intentions. And my cause was just. It was *just*…

Forgetting that he was not alone, in the intensity of his anguish, he brought both fists down on the table with sufficient force to make the glasses tumble over. Having spilled their contents, they rolled to the edge of the table and smashed on the black marble tiles. The sprawling Malick sat bolt upright, exclaiming, 'Cool down, man, cool down. Breaking my glasses won't solve anything-oh.'

'I know, I know,' Kanekeh apologised. 'But the thing is too hard to bear. Anyway, my brother, the reason I came is that I need your help one more time. You are my only hope. I beg you, please arrange a place for me to lose myself with my woman. Anywhere, so long as it is in Africa. I have some diamonds…Take them.'

Wishing now that he had never set eyes on Kanekeh outside his cousin's shop that afternoon, Malick waved away the offer.

'Keep your diamonds. You will need them because finding a place for you to hide won't be easy. As I told you even *I* have to lie low for a while.'

Pushing back his chair, he got to his feet grunting with the effort it took to raise his enormous body, and moved towards the glass doors which led to the veranda from the sitting room. He called out, 'Fanta-ah, Let one of the boys come with a cloth and a broom. Drinks have spilled here. And there is broken glass.'

Kanekeh remained seated for a moment longer, then realising that the discussion had come to an end, reluctantly pushed back his own chair and stood up. He had no idea what his next step would be if Malick would not or could not help him, so it was with a feeling of even deeper depression that he retired to their bedroom, flopped on the bed, and lay staring at nothing. However, his spirits lifted a little the next morning when Malick, in a somewhat better mood, told him that during the night he had remembered a business associate who owed him a favour. He would contact him immediately.

The following exchange of faxes arranged Kanekeh's escape:

'Salt-water Boy,

Warm greetings from that place on the hill. I still remember our adventures in Port Harcourt year before last.

One of my brothers recently suffered a nervous breakdown and his doctor has recommended total rest. I thought of your peaceful island. Can you arrange something for me? His wife will accompany him, but he has more than ample means to pay for their board and lodging.

Regards to your madams,

Paymaster'

'Paymaster,

Salutations from the island. Our adventures in Port Harcourt are still fresh in my mind. Anything for such a good friend. I shall make all arrangements and send for them in ten days time. You can count on me.

Regards,

Salt-water Boy'

Just before dark on the tenth evening after the fugitives' arrival, a nondescript van drew up outside Malick's mansion. The driver went to the tall iron gates, had a word with the guard, then returned to his vehicle to wait. Shortly afterwards, two women descended the front steps, both of them dressed alike with two cloths wrapped around their waists, one on top of the other, loose blouses and head ties, all in the same dark material as if they were going to a funeral. Observers of their descent might have found something strange about the older woman, particularly the way she moved. She seemed unnaturally stiff around the middle for an African woman - as if she were recovering from recent abdominal surgery. Had they continued watching till she hitched up her cloth to climb into the van, they would have noticed that on her feet she had on the type of laced canvas boots that soldiers sometimes wear. But there was no one around to observe the fugitives' secret departure into exile. Not even Malick saw them go down the steps, for he had remained in his sitting-room after saying goodbye in a manner so indifferent that it deepened Kanekeh's depression once more.

The moment the passengers pulled their doors shut the driver, who had no desire to stay longer than was necessary outside the home of a reputed cocaine millionaire, executed an expert manoeuvre and started down the narrow road.

The sound of the revving engine, brought Malick out to the veranda where he remained, rocking morosely back and forth against the wrought iron railing till the van's tail-lights disappeared into the growing darkness. Not until he received another fax a few weeks later did some sparkle return to his eyes.

'Paymaster,

Bad news. Your dear brother is no more and, according to the wishes of his wife, the funeral has already taken place. This is how it happened. Against my advice, he went to town to sell one of his diamonds, thinking he would get a better price than I offered him. Armed robbers came to his place that same night, rightly believing that he had more stones. Your brother had a pistol and there was an exchange of fire. He shot two of them dead, but he himself was hit by a bullet that went right through his neck. We thank God that his lovely wife escaped unharmed and shall continue to look after her. It will be a pleasure to do so.

Sincere condolences.

Salt-water Boy.'

'I knew I could depend on that one to read between the lines,' Malick muttered, chuckling a little. A sly smile still played around his lips as he fed the fax into the paper shredder after replying, *'What a tragedy! Blessings of Allah be upon you, my brother. Best regards. Paymaster.'*

THE END